Contents

Preface

Volumes and volumes have been written about the Vietnam War. It has been the subject of endless discussion and analysis in a variety of media forms. One might ask, Why another book on Vietnam? My answer is that I always have felt that the reasons for our participation in that war were not very well understood, and that is still true today. It is one of the goals of this book to explain the background policies and actions since World War II that made our Vietnam involvement a logical next step in U.S. foreign policy at that time. I also hope to do this in a fashion that is understandable to the average person, but not too simplistic for the person with scholarly or research interests in the subject.

Let me emphasize that this work is in no way an effort to justify *or* criticize U.S. involvement in the Vietnam War but an attempt to show that things occurred in a motivated sequence. Foreign policy evolved according to situations, and as events evolved after World War II the successes and sometimes the things we viewed as our failures in foreign policy led to the logic of U.S. involvement in the war.

The second purpose of this book could tend to be a bit more controversial. The history of the war has been written, for the most part, by those who felt that the war was wrong. Depictions in the movies and other media have consciously or subconsciously imprinted on people's minds certain "givens" about the Vietnam War that are opinion but are going down in history as fact. I will be offering some different analysis on these selected events and "givens" to, I hope, stimulate some reflective, analytical, and objective thinking on the reader's part. It is my hope that this will lead to a more balanced view concerning the war on the part of the mainstream public.

My particular goal is to give Vietnam veterans, their parents, their children and grandchildren, and students of history a working and manageable understanding of U.S. reasons for involvement in the Vietnam War. In addition, readers will have a better working understanding of the sometimes erroneous "givens" that have been associated with that war.

Part I

Introduction

At the end of World War II the world was a vastly changed place. The United States' role in world affairs also had reached a dramatic turning point. No longer would the United States perceive itself to have the privilege of the splendid isolation that it had enjoyed for the majority of its relatively brief history. After the hot war ended, a new kind of war emerged; this was the cold war.

The Union of Soviet Socialist Republics and the United States of America had emerged from World War II as the world's two superpowers. Each represented a different and contending ideology that each country felt should be adopted by the rest of the world's nations. The Soviet Union represented the ideology of totalitarian communism and since its inception in 1917 had espoused the spread of this ideology. The United States remained committed basically to the concepts of democracy as a political system and capitalism (or a variety of other terms for it, such as *market economy*) as the preferred economic system. These ideologies are diametrically opposed to each other, hence the ideological conflict between the two systems and countries as they both attempted to persuade the ex-colonial, newly emerging nations to adopt and embrace their respective systems.

It is the contention of this book that the United States' involvement in the conflict in Vietnam was a logical outgrowth of the foreign policy actions and doctrines that emerged from this ideological struggle called the cold war. Part 1 of this book will attempt to explain some of the major foreign policy doctrines and actions that emerged during this era and how they led the United States along a path that culminated in its involvement in the Vietnam conflict. The doctrines are not intended to be all-encompassing, nor is their explanation intended to justify or impeach the validity of U.S. involvement. It is hoped that the reader will see the logic and gain an understanding of these major foreign policy doctrines.

The areas that will be explored in the following chapters will be: the policy of containment, the Truman Doctrine, the Domino Theory, the development of the Southeast Asia Treaty Organization (SEATO), and the Gulf of Tonkin Incident and Resolution.

As the foreign policy doctrines are explained, an attempt will be made to highlight the most important events leading to America's war in Vietnam and the most important events during America's war in Vietnam. Knowledge of these highlights, I hope, will create important background knowledge for part 2 of this book, when some analytical commentary will be forthcoming about some of the events and attitudes concerning the U.S. war in Vietnam.

1

Containment and the Truman Doctrine

We understand the Russian need to be secure on her western frontiers from all renewal of German aggression. We welcome her to her rightful place among the leading nations of the world. Above all, we welcome constant, frequent, and growing contacts between the Russian people and our own people on both sides of the Atlantic. It is my duty, however, to place before you certain facts about the present position in Europe.

From Stetten in the Baltic to Trieste in the Adriatic, an iron curtain has descended across the continent. Behind that line lie all the capitals of the ancient states of central and eastern Europe.

—Winston Churchill

The speech by Winston Churchill from which this chapter's epigraph has been taken was a defining moment in what was to become the cold war. Many believe that it was the opening verbal salvo of the cold war. The speech, which occurred in Fulton, Missouri, pointed out to citizens of the United States and the world what was happening in Eastern Europe. Soviet troops remained stationed in Europe at the location they had occupied at the end of World War II. It appeared to some that Soviet intentions were to remain in these countries indefinitely and/or until the time that communist governments to their liking were established.

Back in February of 1945 representatives of the Big Three

of World War II, Franklin D. Roosevelt of the United States, Winston Churchill of the United Kingdom, and Josef Stalin of the Union of Soviet Socialist Republics, had met and reached numerous agreements concerning the post–World War II world. It was the perception of the Americans and the British that Stalin had pledged to hold free elections in the Soviet-occupied countries of Eastern Europe. "By the Declaration on Liberated Europe, Roosevelt and Churchill obtained the pledge of Stalin for joint action to secure the fundamental freedoms for the people in territories overrun by the Red Army."[1] The perception that Stalin was in the process of reneging on this promise was reflected in the Churchill's Fulton speech.

As history unfolded during the time period 1945–48 all of the countries of Eastern Europe became Soviet satellites and puppets. The presence and threat of Soviet military might caused the countries of Poland, East Germany, Hungary, Bulgaria, Romania, and Czechoslovakia to adopt pro-Soviet communist governments that existed at the behest of the USSR. Added to this was the fact that early during World War II the Soviet Union had annexed the three Baltic states of Latvia, Lithuania, and Estonia. Yugoslavia by this time also had adopted a communist government, and the United States did not know whether the Yugoslavians would end up in the Soviet orbit also. (They did not.) To the United States these events were ominous. Soviet and communist gains were, to say the least, alarming at this point in history to the United States of America.

A variety of things occurred as a result of what the United States saw as Soviet expansion and imperialism. The Marshall Plan was implemented in 1948 to economically rebuild the nations of Europe. Originally offered to all nations, including those in the Soviet sphere, it primarily rebuilt Western Europe and ensured that an economically devastated area would remain a market and trading partner of the United States. Called an economic miracle, the Marshall Plan helped to rebuild the area of Western Europe and remove it from the category of being ripe for potential communist takeover. Eastern European nations were prohibited by the Soviet Union from participating in the Marshall Plan. Czechoslovakia had previously indicated a desire to participate, but a Soviet-backed communist coup cemented Soviet domination there in 1948.

The North Atlantic Treaty Organization (NATO) was formed in 1949 as the result of a collective security agreement whereby if any of its member nations was attacked all members of the alliance would respond to the attack. The original twelve members of NATO when it was initially formed in 1949 were Belgium, Canada, Denmark, France, Iceland, Italy, Luxembourg, the Netherlands, Norway, Portugal, the United Kingdom, and the United States. By 1952 Greece and Turkey were added to the alliance, and West Germany became a member in 1955. The message sent to the Soviet Union and its satellites by NATO was that any attack by the Soviets or any of their puppets on any NATO member would result in a responsive attack on the Soviet Union by the United States and its NATO allies.

U.S. responses to Soviet expansion such as the Marshall Plan and NATO flowed from foreign policy doctrines that were developed during this post–World War II era in response to the perceived Soviet threat. Chief among these doctrines are the policy of containment and the foreign policy statement known as the Truman Doctrine. These two policies worked in tandem in the attempt to check Soviet expansion. It is these same basic policies and what we perceived as their historic successes that laid the groundwork for U.S. involvement in the Vietnam War. Following will be an examination of the contents of these doctrines and the foreign policy applications where they were perceived as successful. This same perceived success led to the assumption that these foreign policy doctrines could be applied to the situation in Vietnam.

To gain understanding of containment, a working definition of the term is useful. Containment can be defined as

> a general policy adopted in 1947 by the Truman administration to build "situations of strength" around the periphery of the Soviet Union and Eastern Europe in order to contain communist power within its existing boundaries. Underlying the containment policy was a belief that, if Soviet expansion could be stopped, communism would collapse of its own internal weaknesses. The policy was developed by George Kennan and was first applied in the Truman Doctrine of 1947 in a program of military aid to Greece and Turkey.[2]

George Kennan was the architect of the containment policy. Kennan was the head of the State Department's policy-planning staff and an adviser to Secretary of State Dean Acheson. While in that position Kennan wrote a highly influential article under the pseudonym Mr. X that basically outlined U.S. foreign policy assumptions at the beginning of the cold war. In the article the idea of containment first appeared. Kennan wrote: "We have seen how deeply that concept [of the innate antagonism between capitalism and socialism] has become imbedded in the foundations of Soviet power. It has profound implications for Russia's conduct as a member of international society. It means there can never be on Moscow's side any sincere assumption of a community of aims between the Soviet Union and the powers which are regarded as capitalist."[3] Kennan then writes what is to become the policy: "In these circumstances it is clear that the main element of any United States policy toward the Soviet Union must be that of a long-term, patient but firm and vigilant containment of Russian expansive tendencies."[4] Kennan believed at the time that the confrontation with the Soviet Union was to be a long-term affair. "The

Russians look forward to a duel of infinite duration, and they see that they already have scored great successes."[5]

These perceived Soviet successes and advances in the world caused the United States to move to vast new programs to implement the containment policy. The United States began to rearm itself, establish treaties of mutual defense with other countries, and sought to establish military bases around the world. If a person were to take a look at a polar map projection of the world, it would appear that the United States and its alliances were encircling the Soviet Union. That was the goal, to encircle communism and keep it within its existing boundaries.

All of this was a clear cut departure from traditional U.S. foreign policy. "Throughout most of American History, President George Washington's advice to 'steer clear of permanent alliances' was carefully observed."[6] Washington had enunciated this policy in his farewell address in 1796, and it had been the cornerstone of U.S. foreign policy until the post–World War II era. The United States went from avoiding permanent alliances to seeking them. After World War II, the United States became party to over forty permanent alliances. NATO has already been mentioned and has always been America's primary alliance. Other major alliances entered into included the Rio Treaty, which is a collective defense pact for the Western Hemisphere; ANZUS, a mutual defense treaty for Australia, New Zealand, and the United States; the Baghdad Pact, which later became known as CENTO; and SEATO, which had a direct impact on our involvement in Vietnam. The United States also was party to many bilateral treaties, including treaties with South Korea, Japan, and the Philippines. The United States was not to become isolationist again and basically took on the position as the primary opponent to communist expansion in the world.

The Truman Doctrine was, of course, the blood brother of the containment policy. An explanation of the policy follows:

9

The policy, adopted by President Harry Truman in 1947, called for the support for all free peoples resisting armed subjugation by internal or outside forces. The policy was aimed expressly at halting communist expansion in southeastern Europe and was expounded in a speech to Congress in which President Truman asked for an appropriation of $400 million for military and economic aid to Greece and Turkey. The doctrine was linked with the policy of "containment" that called for the building of "situations of strength" around the periphery of communist power.[7]

"The Truman Doctrine marked the official acceptance of the 'containment' philosophy of building up free world strength to halt communist expansionism."[8] The policy, though enunciated by Truman primarily for southeastern Europe, was accepted by succeeding presidents and deemed to be applicable in other areas of the world. The idea that the United States would help free peoples to resist subjugation by internal or external forces played out in America's involvement in Vietnam. As mentioned, the Truman Doctrine and the policy of containment went hand in hand. "American actions in Korea and South Vietnam were based on the policy of containing communist power."[9]

Evidence suggested to U.S. policy makers that the policy of containment and the Truman Doctrine were achieving some success in the quest to limit the expansion of communism. Areas of the world that supported this conclusion were Greece and Turkey in Western Europe, and the Asian hot spot of South Korea.

Britain had long been the guardian of Western interests in the Mediterranean. After World War II Britain was not in any position militarily or economically to continue in that role. The problem was that by 1947 the Soviet Union was demanding of Turkey to give up control of the Dardenelles, which is the strategic waterway that links the Black Sea and the Mediterranean Sea. Added to this, Greek communist insurgents were attempting to overthrow the anti-communist government in Greece. U.S. foreign policy makers believed that the insurgents in Greece were aided by and took their orders from the Soviet Union. The fear in the United States was that Soviet control of the Dardenelles and of Greece would lead to, among other things, Soviet dominance of the Suez Canal, which would have immediate, obvious negative consequences regarding resource access to Middle Eastern oil.

The power vacuum that had been created by the British departure in the Mediterranean was filled by the United States under the newly enunciated Truman Doctrine. U.S. aid flowed to Greece and Turkey to bolster the military forces of those two countries. The communist insurgents capitulated in Greece, giving up the struggle by October 1949. With the strengthening of the Turkish military, the Dardenelles also remained under the control of Turkey.

Foreign policy makers in the United States saw the successes in Greece and Turkey as victories in the cold war. The conclusion drawn was that the Truman Doctrine and the policy of containment had effectively stopped Soviet-inspired attempts at expansionism. This "lesson" was imprinted in the minds of U.S. foreign policy makers and became a mainstay of U.S. foreign policy thinking to be used in the future.

At the conclusion of World War II the peninsula of Korea had been occupied by Soviet forces in the north and U.S. forces in the south. The dividing line between the two forces was the thirty-eighth parallel of latitude. Both countries had agreed earlier to form a unified government for Korea at a later date. Growing suspicions between the United States and the Soviet Union, caused by the events that were the cold war, prevented this unification. By 1948 North Korea and South Korea had set up separate governments, both of which claimed the authority to rule the entire country. South Korea called itself the Republic of Korea, was supported by the United States, and was recognized as the country's lawful government by thirty members of the United Nations. North Korea was controlled by a communist government, called itself the People's Republic of Korea, and was supported by the Soviet Union.

The Soviets withdrew from North Korea in 1948, leaving the North Korean army well armed. The Americans withdrew from South Korea in 1949. On June 25, 1950, North Korea launched a full-scale invasion of South Korea. On June 27, 1950, President Truman pledged U.S. aid for the defense of South Korea. On the evening of June 27 the UN Security Council labeled North Korea as the aggressor and called upon member nations to come to the defense of South Korea. Eventually sixteen member nations were contributing to the defense of South Korea. The UN forces were placed under the command of U.S. general Douglas MacArthur. While this was considered a UN action, the greatest burden of the defense of South Korea fell upon the United States, which contributed most of the air and sea power and about half of the ground forces. (South Korea contributed the greatest part of the remainder of the ground forces.) Other large contributors to the war effort were Australia, Canada, Great Britain, and Turkey.

The day after the North Korean invasion, President Truman went to Blair House in Washington, D.C., for a meeting of top officials concerning the Korean crisis. "All assumed without question that Russia had engineered the attack, using North Korean stooge forces to probe for a soft spot in the American containment shield. Here was a test of American will and power. Worse yet, they speculated, the thrust in Korea might be only one component of a worldwide communist assault. Would Yugoslavia be next? Iran? Formosa? Indochina? The Philippines? Japan? Germany?"[10]

The United States interpreted the North Korean attack on

the South as an occurrence of Soviet communist expansionism. The United States successfully brought the issue to the United Nations and successfully maneuvered them into translating U.S. foreign policy aims into UN policy.

The war itself went very poorly for the UN forces in the early going. UN forces were driven back to the small southeastern corner of the Korean peninsula called the Pusan Perimeter by early September of 1950. By the middle of September, however, UN forces were ready for a counteroffensive which they launched successfully with the Inchon landing on September 15, 1950. This was coupled with a simultaneous breakout by UN forces from the Pusan Perimeter. This counteroffensive was so successful that by October 1, 1950, the North Koreans had been pushed out of South Korea and UN forces were sitting just to the south of the thirty-eighth parallel.

On October 7, 1950, the United Nations passed a resolution authorizing the UN forces to attack to the north of the thirty-eighth parallel. It was concluded that the long-standing goal of unifying the Koreas was to be achieved by the defeat of North Korea. No longer were UN forces merely to defend the South but to move north. The UN forces moved north and took the North Korean capital of Pyongyang on October 19, 1950. The UN forces pushed farther north approaching the Yalu River and the border with China. (In China the communists had taken power in 1949 after a long civil war with the nationalists, who then fled to the island of Formosa [Taiwan].)

Communist China changed the nature of the war by intervening and driving the UN forces back to the south of the thirty-eighth parallel by January of 1951. There then were thrusts and counterthrusts until June, 1951, and by that time battle lines had stabilized near the thirty-eighth parallel. For the remainder of the war both sides dug into the hills and waged a frequently violent war over outposts between their respective lines.

13

On July 27, 1953, an armistice was signed that ended the fighting. Politically and militarily the war's results were inconclusive. Relations between the United States and Communist China were worsened by the war. The United States had not yet granted China diplomatic recognition, and this became less likely as a result of the war. The policy of containment and the Truman Doctrine had previously consisted of political and economic measures including economic aid to resist communists and their expansionism. Containment, with the Korean War, had taken on a military dimension including U.S. military participation with ground forces to stop communism. The "lesson" learned and noted in Korea was again, however, that containment worked. The sovereignty and noncommunist status of South Korea had been preserved. Communism met with stern measures could be stopped in its tracks successfully.

Chinese participation in the Korean War fed the U.S. perception that all communist countries were a monolithic bloc. U.S. perception was that all communist countries acted in unison and that direction for all communist activities originated in the Soviet Union, was assisted by the Chinese, and filtered down to communist movements in the developing countries. Communist movements, such as those in Indochina, were perceived by U.S. foreign policy makers as part of the international communist movement, and this perception had ramifications for U.S. policy in Southeast Asia.

France had successfully placed Indochina (Laos, Cambodia, and Vietnam) under colonial rule in their empire by the 1890s. During World War II all of Southeast Asia was conquered and became part of the Japanese empire. Local populations took note of the fact that the Asian, yellow-skinned Japanese had taken power from the former European, white, and supposedly superior colonial masters. When the Japanese were defeated, local leaders made moves to take back control of their countries. "In August of 1945, Ho Chi Minh proclaimed

14

Vietnam to be a free, united, and independent nation, and he called upon other members of the world community to acknowledge this fact."[11] European countries, such as France, had other ideas. The Europeans intended to return to their former colonies and reimposed colonial control. This was the case of the French in Indochina. The origin of the conflict in Vietnam was rooted in the struggle between Vietnamese that wanted to take control of their country and the French, who wanted to reimpose colonial control.

The United States, it seemed, would take an anti-colonialist position. "As President Roosevelt bluntly put it: 'I can't believe that we can fight a war against fascist slavery and at the same time not work to free people from all over the world from colonial policy.'"[12] Roosevelt had also given his opinion on whether France should reimpose rule on Indochina. "Declaring more than once that Indochina should not be returned to France after the war, Roosevelt explained, 'France has had the country—thirty million inhabitants—for nearly one hundred years, and the people are worse off than they were at the beginning.'"[13] As events unfolded in the post–World War II world, the United States moved slowly from an anticolonialist to an indifferent, and finally to a pro-French policy concerning France's involvement in Vietnam. The factors and events that caused this change will be examined.

In Vietnam, Ho Chi Minh and the French initially negotiated to determine what type of government and under whose auspices Vietnam would be ruled. It seemed at first that the agreement was to be that there would be a Republic of Vietnam with a parliament and army and control over its own finances. It was to be, however, part of a French Indochinese Federation. This probably meant that the French would have control over foreign affairs. It did not matter, however, as the contending parties could not hammer out the specific details and war broke out in 1946 between the French and the Vietminh (a group of communists and nationalists that had been formed to resist Japanese occupation during World War II and later led the struggle against the French). In the early going the French were able to gain the large cities as strongholds and the Vietminh retreated to the countryside and began the long struggle known as the First Indochinese War.

While the war went on in Indochina between the French and the Vietminh, that area of the world was somewhat peripheral to American concerns from 1945 to 1949. Center stage of American foreign policy at that time was Europe and Japan, rebuilding to make them viable members of the international capitalist trading community. In Europe particularly the goal was to strengthen the countries for the economic reason of making them trade partners. As the countries of Europe became stronger, as has been mentioned earlier, they would also become strong military partners of the United States to resist the expansion of Soviet communism.

> Given America's concern for France's pivotal role in European recovery, it seemed prudent to set aside America's marginal anticolonialism; refrain from erecting any barriers to French actions in Indochina; and indulge only in occasional sermonettes to the French about giving the "natives" more responsibilities. Indeed, that was the essence of American policy between 1946 and 1949 as France sought to reintegrate Indochina into the French empire in the face of determined opposition from the Vietminh. [14]

U.S. policy gave greater priority to a strong France in a strong postwar Europe than to the aspirations of the Vietnamese. Containment of the Soviets in Europe took precedence over all other matters at this point. President Truman had refused to answer pleas by Ho Chi Minh for some kind of diplomatic recognition for his government. The United States took a role of nominal noninterference at this point. This policy allowed the United States to retain an anticolonialist stance while simultaneously doing nothing to interfere with French colonialism. The net effect of this was not neutral and, in fact, strengthened the French position and effort. In fact, the United States somewhat looked the other way as the French used Marshall Plan aid to further their colonial adventures. "So even before the first formalization of aid in the spring of 1950, the United States looked the other way while France used surplus American military equipment and Marshall Plan dollars to fight and finance her war. Still, American aid was indirect, its commitment limited and cautious, and its sense of Indochina's importance ephermal and contingent on France's role in Europe."[15]

In the early part of the struggle the French enjoyed advantages of superior manpower and firepower. Their strategy was to lure the Vietminh into a conventional battle, where the French could use their conventional advantages to defeat the Vietminh. The Vietminh turned out to be a wily opponent that would not play into the French hands. They preferred hit-and-run guerrilla tactics that emanated from the Vietminh commander Gen. Vo Nguyen Giap. Giap intended to continue guerrilla war until he could build up a modern army with the weapons necessary to give the French the type of battle they desired, but on his terms. In time Giap was able to increase the size of his army from 50,000 to about 350,000.

The other war that was occurring in Vietnam was for the support of the people. The advantage the Vietminh had in this area was the leadership of the charismatic Ho Chi Minh. The French tried to counter this with a political offensive of their own. They provided anticommunist Vietnamese nationalists a leader of their own in the personage of Emperor Bao Dai. In June of 1949, the French granted limited independence to what they called the state of Vietnam within the French Union. Bao Dai was the chief of state, and the government did have some internal autonomy and an army of its own. The French, however, retained strong powers to protect French nationals and their economic interests. Foreign policy was coordinated with the policy of France. The French appointment of Bao Dai was also designed to convince Americans that they were willing to extend a degree of independence to Vietnam.

In 1949 it was clear that two competing governments were present in Vietnam. Ho Chi Minh had declared his government, the Democratic Republic of Vietnam (DRV), to be the legitimate rulers of Vietnam, and the anticommunist nationalists had a different government under Bao Dai and the French.

In 1949 events occurred that changed the war in Indochina from a struggle for independence of a colony from its colonial master into a battlefield of the cold war. The initial event that set off the chain that followed was the victory of Mao Zedong and his communists over the nationalists in China in late 1949. The communist victory drove the noncommunist forces, which had battled the communists in a long civil war, to the island of Taiwan. In the United States this was perceived as a great setback to the anticommunist cause that they had championed. The world's greatest landmass, Asia, was dominated by communist governments in the world's largest country (Soviet Union) and the world's most populous country (China). The United States, as you recall, perceived communism as a monolithic, expansionary mass, and the success of Mao in China reinforced this notion.

For the French, communist successes in China allowed Paris to claim to be fighting a war of containment, thus reassuring the United States of the strategic importance of Indochina and France's commitment there. The "loss of China" confirmed Washington's belief in a Chinese-Soviet threat in Indochina. When Russia and China extended diplomatic recognition to the DRV in January 1950, Secretary of State Dean Acheson claimed that this removed "any illusions as to the 'nationalist' nature of Ho Chi Minh's aims and [revealed] Ho in his true col-

ors as the mortal enemy of native independence in Indochina."
The United States countered with the recognition of Bao Dai
and the State of Vietnam. The State of Vietnam was now seen
as the key to the defense of Southeast Asia. Direct military and
economic aid was forthcoming.[16]

In early 1950, after North Vietnam began to receive assistance from China, offensive action was initiated against French
Union Forces, which were composed of French and Vietnamese soldiers. In the meantime, Ho Chi Minh rid his coalition
government of moderates and nationalists whom he had accepted earlier, and showed himself to be completely communist. In March 1951 the Indochinese Communist Party, which
had been dissolved in 1945, was revived as the Workers Party
of Lac Dong.[17]

The events that had occurred in China and the actions of Ho
Chi Minh and his DRV were placed into context of the aggressive actions of communist North Korea in 1950 and appeared
to U.S. foreign policy analysts as part of a well-woven communist conspiracy for world domination. The French reinforced
this view in their arguments and their requests for economic
and military assistance. By May of 1950 the United States had
decided to give aid to the Bao Dai government through the
French. The die was cast. The United States was to give support to the French and the Vietnamese that were considered by
the United States anticommunist nationalists. The United
States believed that the struggle in Indochina was part of the
worldwide struggle against monolithic international communism and the way to meet the challenge was through containment in Indochina. "There now existed two Vietnams—each
sporting powerful Cold War allies. The war of resistance, begun
as a localized struggle against French imperial rule, had now
become a major front in the Cold War."[18]
American aid to the French, which began in 1950, in-

creased steadily through 1954, by which time the United States was bearing about four-fifths of the French costs for the struggle. The French for their part were beginning to tire of the war as it dragged on. Their military situation had scarcely improved in the years 1950–54, and the domestic political situation back in France was demanding some decisive action. The French general Navarre decided to increase the mobility of the French forces by using the Vietnamese forces (anticommunist) to take over defensive positions. The French then hoped to lure the Vietminh into a set-piece battle and win a decisive victory.

The place eventually chosen to do this was a flat valley surrounded by hills called Dien Bien Phu. The place chosen was on a major Vietminh supply route, and the French felt it played to their strengths. The French felt they could set up headquarters in the center and ring the valley with fortifications which would allow them to have their guns fixed on the surrounding hills. The French would be resupplied and reinforced by an airstrip located near headquarters. Their strategy was to draw the forces of the Vietminh under General Giap into human wave attacks on their fortified positions and cut them to pieces.

The French made some fatal calculations about their enemy. The Vietminh had developed into a modernized, well-disciplined army that was better-armed, with more sophisticated Soviet and Chinese weapons, than anticipated. The Vietminh, with massive use of human muscle, succeeded in dragging their artillery pieces up the steep slopes and were able to keep the artillery and their troops resupplied as the battle unfolded. Vietminh artillery could strike the French positions at will.

The French had begun moving into Dien Bien Phu in November of 1953 and were well settled when the siege began. The attack began on March 13, 1954, with a massive Vietminh artillery barrage. Artillery barrages were followed by Vietminh ground attacks that successfully captured two outer French fortifications within three days and a third by the seventeenth day. The airstrip was rendered useless for reinforcement and resupply, so the French had to rely on resupply and reinforcement by parachute drop, which also became increasingly ineffective.

Conditions continued to deteriorate at Dien Bien Phu, and there was some discussion of U.S. military intervention to alleviate the situation. There had been talk of a U.S. air strike to relieve the siege at Dien Bien Phu. American president Dwight D. Eisenhower said that he would authorize an air strike only if he had congressional approval. Congressional leaders said approval would be forthcoming only if the strike were part of a multinational effort. Great Britain would not give their approval to the effort, nor would the French agree to the multinational nature of a military relief effort. France would agree to a unilateral U.S. air strike but feared if any effort was multinational they would lose control of their decision-making power over the Indochinese issue.

Due to this lack of consensus, military relief was not forthcoming. The siege lasted fifty-six days. The Vietminh advanced relentlessly before the French were finally overrun and defeated. They had been outnumbered ten to one, which they had not anticipated. The final French stronghold was taken on May 8, 1954. "In the Battle of Dien Bien Phu the French suffered 7,693 casualties: 2,080 killed in action, 5,613 wounded. Another 1,606 men were listed as missing in action, and 6,500 became prisoners of war."[19] The French suffered a massive military defeat and Dien Bien Phu marked the end, for all purposes, of their colonial effort in Indochina.

During the siege of Dien Bien Phu there had already been agreement by the Big Four powers (United States, Great Britain, Soviet Union, and France) to include discussion at a conference in Geneva to settle the situation in Indochina. The outcome of the battle, of course, altered some bargaining positions of certain parties once the conference convened. During the siege and the discussions of military relief of the siege, the concept of a collective security agreement to protect Southeast Asia from communism was broached. While not doing anything to assist the French at Dien Bien Phu, this concept later led to the development of SEATO, which will be discussed later in this book. The concept of dominoes falling was also broached at this momentous time. This, of course, conjures up thoughts of the Domino Theory, which will be also discussed later and has ramifications for U.S. involvement in the Vietnam War.

U.S. efforts at containment in Indochina at this point had merely consisted of giving aid to the French in their effort to stop what Americans viewed as the communist forces in Vietnam. There was no U.S. military involvement at this point. The defeat of the French, however, left a power vacuum in Indochina in the struggle against communism. That power vacuum would be filled eventually by the United States.

This chapter has been an effort to show the reader how the Truman Doctrine and the containment policy were initially brought about by perceived communist Soviet expansionist tendencies. The doctrines pledged to help free peoples resist inwardly or outwardly imposed tyrannies and were seen to be applied successfully in Greece, Turkey, and Korea, where the United States perceived Soviet-inspired communist threats. When China became communist, the U.S. perception of monolithic, expansionist communism that was directed from the Soviet Union and filtered through China was reinforced. Furthermore, through a series of events in Indochina, the United States came to believe that Ho Chi Minh and his Democratic Republic of Vietnam were agents of the spread of international monolithic communism. This necessitated, in U.S.

eyes, actions taken that were in line with the Truman Doctrine and the policy of containment. These policies then became key stepping-stones that led the United States down the path of its later involvement in the Vietnam War.

Notes

1. Testimony of Averill Harriman, Hearings before the Senate Committee on Armed Services and the Senate Committee on Foreign Relations, Eighty-second Congress, First Session, *Military Situation in the Far East,* Washington, D.C., 1951, pp. 3328–41.
2. Jack C. Plano and Milton Greenberg, *The American Political Dictionary,* Orlando, FL: Holt, Rhinehart and Winston, 1989, p. 476.
3. George F. Kennan, "The Sources of Soviet Conduct," *Foreign Affairs* 25 (July 1947), reprinted in Howard R. Anderson, ed., *A History of the United States with Selected Readings* (Boston: Houghton Mifflin, 1970), p. 617.
4. Ibid., p. 618.
5. Ibid.
6. Plano and Greenberg, *The American Political Dictionary,* p. 468.
7. Ibid., p. 514.
8. Ibid.
9. Ibid., p. 476.
10. Thomas G. Paterson, J. Garry Clifford, and Kenneth L. Hagan, *American Foreign Policy: A History* (Lexington, MA: D. C. Heath, 1977), p. 472.
11. Tony Murdoch, Joan M. Crouse, and Pam O'Connell, *Vietnam* (White Plains, NY: Longman, 1994), p. 24.
12. Ibid., p. 25.
13. Ibid., p. 26.
14. William Appleman Williams, Thomas McCormick, Lloyd Gardner, Walter LeFeber, *America in Vietnam, a Documentary History* (New York: Anchor Press/Doubleday, 1985), p. 47.
15. Ibid., p. 48.
16. Murdoch, Crouse, and O'Connell, *Vietnam,* p. 33.
17. Harry G. Summers, Jr., *Vietnam War Almanac* (New York: Facts on File, 1985), p. 23.
18. Murdoch, Crouse, and O'Connell, *Vietnam,* p. 33.
19. Ibid., p. 40.

2

SEATO and the Domino Theory

As mentioned in the previous chapter, a conference had been convened in Geneva in early 1954. This big-power conference was to meet ostensibly to discuss the situations in Korea and in Berlin. At the request of the French, the question of the Indochina war was to be included on the agenda at the conference. The conference was to include China along with the Soviet Union, United States, Great Britain, and France.

France, when it originally had the Indochina question placed on the agenda, had harbored some hope of salvaging a part of its Asian empire. Military reality, as reflected in the reality of Dien Bien Phu, eliminated this French illusion.

It is important to note that representatives of the French Union (State of Vietnam) were present at the conference and claimed to be the legitimate government of Vietnam. The DRV had its representatives present at Geneva also and considered itself the lawful government of Vietnam. As history unfolds, these respective entities became the basis for separate South Vietnamese and North Vietnamese governments.

The talks at the conference resulted in the Geneva Accords by July 20 and 21, 1954. "The terms of the Vietnamese armistice—controversial from the beginning—provided for a temporary partition of the country at the 17th parallel, evacuation of French forces from the North, a ban on increasing any military materiel in either part of the country, the creation of an international control commission, and the organization of elections to reunify the country before the deadline of July 20, 1956."[1] Under the Geneva Agreement, the Vietminh were to relocate to the north of the seventeenth parallel, while the French Union (State of Vietnam supporters) forces were to relocate to the south of the seventeenth parallel. This evacuation and relocation was to occur within 300 days. The partition of Vietnam was to be temporary. As we shall see, reunification was not to occur as easily as some had envisioned. The immediate result of the partition was the mass exodus of millions of anticommunists from the north to the south and hundreds of thousands of Vietminh and their families from the south to the north. To the Vietminh who went north, the journey was believed to be temporary, as they intended to return south after reunification elections. "Not all Vietminh withdrew to the North after the Geneva conference. Ho and the Communist leadership left in the South in covert status an estimated 8,000 to 10,000 military and civilian cadres."[2] These stay-behinds became an integral part of what Americans referred to later as the Vietcong.

Prior to the convening of the Geneva conference and even prior to the French defeat in Indochina, Pres. Dwight D. Eisenhower's secretary of state, John Foster Dulles, had been actively pursuing the goal of establishing a collective security agreement for the area of Southeast Asia. The result of this effort was the development of SEATO. The SEATO agreement was signed September 8, 1954, at Manila in the Philippines and became part of the legal basis for the United States' involvement in the Vietnam War. SEATO was "an alliance concluded in 1954 aimed at providing security from communist aggression for the Southeast Asian region. Parties to the alliance, who agreed to consult about potential collective action whenever any of them is threatened by external aggression or internal subversion, are Australia, Britain, France, New Zealand, Pakistan, the Philippines, Thailand, and the United

States."[3] "South Vietnam, Laos, and Cambodia were barred from becoming members under the terms of the Geneva armistice agreements, yet Secretary Dulles explained that a protocol to the Geneva Pact extended an 'umbrella' to those three nations."[4]

With the signing of the agreement, the United States was sending a message that it intended to ignore the election and reunification clause of Vietnam armistice. In the SEATO agreement protocol, the description *State of Vietnam* was used explicitly. *State of Vietnam* refers to the South, and this choice of terminology implied that the United States was thinking of the division at the seventeenth parallel as permanent, as opposed to a temporary situation. The signing of the SEATO treaty also signaled the removal of the war in Indochina as an anticolonial struggle and placed it in U.S. thinking as part of the cold war. In U.S. policy thinking, Indochina was now framed as part of the struggle against communism. The reference in the SEATO treaty to defending against external aggression and internal subversion set the stage for labeling the North (DRV) as the aggressor against, and promoter of, internal subversion within the South that necessitated countermeasures under the provisions of the SEATO Treaty.

Discussions in Geneva and the resulting Geneva Accords concerning Indochina were the targets of U.S. skepticism and lack of support from the beginning. The United States did not even sign the Geneva Accords and thereby did not feel it would be bound by its provisions in the future. "Privately the National Security Council (NSC) concluded that the accords were a 'disaster' that 'completed a major forward stride of Communism which may lead to the loss of Southeast Asia.'"[5]

Secretary of State John Foster Dulles had enunciated the U.S. perception concerning the struggle in Indochina in March 1954, and this perception dictated the view that the United States would maintain before and after the Geneva Accords:

The Communists are attempting to prevent the orderly development of independence and to confuse the issue before the world. The Communists have, in these matters, a regular line which Stalin laid down in 1924.

The scheme is to whip up the spirit of nationalism so that it becomes violent. That is done by professional agitators. Then the violence is enlarged by Communist military and technical leadership and the provision of military supplies. In these ways, international Communism gets a strangle hold on the people and it uses that power to "amalgamate" the peoples into the Soviet orbit. "Amalgamazation" is Lenin's and Stalin's word to describe their process.

"Amalgamazation" is now being attempted in Indochina under the ostensible leadership of Ho Chi Minh.[6]

The United States intended to have things two ways. It paid lip service to supporting the Geneva Accords superficially but maneuvered into a position of nonsupport for the provisions of the accords, particularly concerning the reunification elections that the accords mandated. "America's position was to support the unification of divided countries through free elections supervised by the United Nations to ensure that they are conducted fairly. The fact that the Geneva Accords did not require UN supervision of the elections gave the United States reason to refuse signing them and thus keep its options open."[7]

The Geneva Accords themselves were far from a coherent manifesto. They consisted, in part, of a hodgepodge of declarations that included six unilateral declarations and three bilateral declarations, as well as one unsigned declaration. "What it all amounted to was a way of ending hostilities, partitioning Vietnam, and leaving the political outcome to the future."[8]

While the United States allowed the election issues to go to the back burner and the vagaries of the future, there were other matters that elicited a very concrete foreign policy statement concerning the Geneva Accords. " 'At the same time,' the statement warned, 'it would view any renewal of the aggression in violation of the aforesaid arrangements with grave concern and as seriously threatening international peace and security.' "[9] The United States placed itself in a position to circumvent some provisions of the Geneva Accords and enforce other provisions simultaneously.

During the months following the Geneva Conference, the United States made moves to establish a friendly, noncommunist, and permanent South Vietnam. These movements included machinations to establish a new premier for South Vietnam, Ngo Dinh Diem, and posturing for avoidance of reunification elections that were to have occurred in 1956.

The majority of U.S. foreign policy actions concerning Vietnam obviously flowed from our fear of international communism. This fear was embodied in a theory that evolved and coexisted with SEATO, the Domino Theory. As with other doctrines that have been examined, the Domino Theory became one of the key foreign policy doctrines that precipitated our military involvement in the Vietnam War.

In 1952, a National Security council formalized the Domino theory and gave it a sweeping character. Describing a military attack on Indochina as a danger "inherent in the existence of a hostile and aggressive Communist China," it argued that the loss of even a single Southeast Asian country would lead "to relatively swift submission to or an alignment with communism by the remainder. Furthermore, an alignment with communism of the rest of Southeast Asia and India, and in the longer term, of the middle east (with the possible exceptions of at least Pakistan and Turkey) would in all probability progressively follow."[10]

Philosophically, the framework had been set for U.S. foreign policy planning concerning Southeast Asia. This falling dominoes concept molded American policy into support for the French during their military effort in Southeast Asia. About a month before the decisive defeat of the French at Dien Bien Phu, the Domino Theory was publicly enunciated by President Eisenhower at a press conference on April 7, 1954:

Q. Robert Richards, Copley Press: Mr. President, would you mind commenting on the strategic importance of Indochina to the free world? I think there has been, across the country, some lack of understanding on just what it means to us.

The President: You have, of course, both the specific and the general when you talk about such things.

First of all, you have the specific value of a locality in its production of materials the world needs.

Then you have the possibility that many human beings pass under a dictatorship that is inimical to the free world.

Finally, you have broader considerations that might follow what you might call the "falling domino" principle. You have a row of dominoes set up, you knock over the first one, and what will happen to the last one is the certainty that it will go over very quickly. So you could have a beginning of a disintegration that would have the most profound influences.

Now, with respect to the first one, two of the items from this particular area that the world uses are tin and tungsten. They are very important. There are others, of course, the rubber plantations and so on.

Then with respect to more people passing under this domination, Asia, after all, has already lost some 450 million of its people to the Communist dictatorship, and we simply can't afford greater losses.

But when we come to the possible sequence of events, the loss of Indochina, of Burma, of Thailand, of the peninsula, and Indonesia following, now you begin to talk about areas that not only multiply the disadvantages that you would suffer through the loss of materials, sources of materials, but now you are talking about millions and millions and millions of people.

Finally, the geographical position achieved thereby does many things. It turns the so-called island defensive chain of Japan, Formosa, of the Philippines and to the southward; it moves in to threaten Australia and New Zealand.

It takes away, in its economic aspects, that region that Japan must have as a trading area or Japan, in turn, will have only one place in the world to go—that is, toward the Communist areas in order to live.

So, the possible consequences of the loss are just incalculable to the free world.[11]

It would be extremely difficult to find a more succinctly stated rationale and explanation of perceived U.S. vital interest in an area of the world than the treatise that Eisenhower gave at this press conference concerning our interest in Indochina.

The Domino Theory has been expounded periodically since 1954 by top American leaders who used it as justification for military programs in Southeast Asia. Originally applied to all of Indochina, the doctrine was subsequently linked to South Vietnam as the key state in the region by the Johnson administration, which intervened in the latter half of the 1960s with over one-half million troops to keep that "first domino" from falling. Supporters of the Domino Theory argued that a communist victory would mean that American alliance guarantees for other small nations would no longer be credible, and a series of communist victories could be expected.[12]

Communist intentions in the world after World War II were perceived by the United States to be a drive for world dominance. Containment of the communists became the uppermost goal of U.S. foreign policy. The containment policy found its basic premises expressed in the Domino Theory, which was enunciated in reference to the geographical area of Southeast Asia. It was believed that events in that area of the world would have repercussions and a worldwide ripple effect concerning the East–West struggle of the cold war. As the Domino Theory neatly fit into the framework of containment, it also led to the creation of SEATO. SEATO became one of the legal premises to implement containment and attempt to prevent the Domino Theory from occurring. Given the U.S. belief in containment and the Domino Theory as well as the U.S. belief that its credibility to other small nation alliances was contingent upon preventing falling dominoes and communism in Indochina, it is not surprising that U.S. policy during the time period of 1956–64 developed the way it did. More than not being surprising, future involvement in Vietnam is a very *logical* outcome considering evolution of U.S. foreign policy in context of the cold war. Top-level U.S. leaders, including the president himself, placed vital strategic importance to the area of Southeast Asia. By the end of this time period, in 1964, the United States felt that it was pledged to the defense of Southeast Asia in a fashion that was near to equal that of Western Europe. Lyndon Johnson was president by that time, and he felt that the United States had a commitment to the defense of South Vietnam.

> The implication was that the SEATO treaty required the United States to intervene militarily in Vietnam, and although this claim would be convincingly challenged by critics later on, the point is that Johnson himself saw no essential difference, whether legal or political or moral, between the American commitment to the defense of Western Europe against "direct aggression" by the Soviet Union and the defense of the countries of Southeast Asia, including Vietnam, against (in the words of the SEATO treaty) "armed attack and . . . subversive activities directed from without against their territorial integrity and political stability."[13]

It is instructive to discuss the major events as they unfold between 1956 and 1964 to understand the eventual massive U.S. commitment to the Vietnam War.

By June 17, 1954, the emperor Bao Dai had appointed Ngo Dinh Diem as prime minister of South Vietnam and the United States was pledged to the success and the development of Diem's regime in South Vietnam. The United States' desire was "in developing and maintaining a strong, viable state, capable of resisting attempted subversion or aggression through military means."[14] To accomplish this, the United States would have to pour in military and economic aid in massive amounts, as well as train a South Vietnamese army. "It also involved acquiescing in Diem's refusal to honor the provision of the Geneva Accords calling for national elections in 1956 to unify the country."[15] The question of who was primarily responsible for torpedoing reunification elections is controversial and will be elaborated on elsewhere in this book. Diem's refusal and U.S. backing of the refusal cast the die for the ensuing struggle in Vietnam.

Diem by 1956 had begun an era of political repression and campaign of terror to root out dissidents and communists. His government used heavy-handed tactics against various sects, including Buddhists (who were a much larger group than Diem and the Catholics) and the communists. These repressive tactics grew worse and lasted throughout Diem's time in power. This naturally undermined the strength of the South Vietnamese regime under Diem and alienated a great number of Southerners. It was very difficult to wage a struggle with the communists with Diem alienating much of the noncommunist populace as well.

U.S. military advisory efforts had originated back in 1950, when Southeast Asia was still Indochina under the French.

This "military mission" was the U.S. Military Assistance Advisory Group (MAAG) Indochina, which was established in Saigon on September 17, 1950. After the formation of South Vietnam, known officially as the Republic of Vietnam (RVN) by the Geneva Accords in 1954, the title was changed to MAAG-Vietnam. Advisory teams were first assigned to South Vietnam's Joint General Staff, Defense Ministry, Army, Navy and Air Force, then to military schools, training centers and Army Divisions as well. Their mission included combat arms training for the South Vietnamese Armed Forces (SVNAF) and, as MAAG strength increased, provincial and regimental advisors were assigned to South Vietnamese units in the field. There were some 900 military advisors in Indochina when President Dwight D. Eisenhower left office in 1961. By 1963, under President John F. Kennedy, the figure had risen to 16,300.[16]

Communist activity during the period 1956–59 consisted mainly of political struggle and minor insurgent activity against the Diem regime in South Vietnam while Diem continued his campaign against communists, Buddhists, and the sects such as the Cao Dai, Hoa Hao, and Binh Xuyen. These sects had sustained serious damage by Diem's forces. Nineteen fifty-nine marked a turning point in Vietnam as the communists moved to turn the struggle into a full-scale guerrilla war. This was the beginning of what the United States came to know as the Vietcong:

> Vietcong was a derogatory term for Vietnamese communists in the south. At the end of the war between the French and Vietminh (1946–54) 90,000 Vietminh troops in what was to become South Vietnam were repatriated to the north. But the Vietminh left behind an estimated 5,000 to 10,000 soldiers as a fifth column in the south. Instructed by Hanoi to lie low until 1959, they were then activated by the North Vietnamese Politburo to begin a guerrilla war in the south to subvert and overthrow the standing government.[17]

Stepped-up activity was not to be limited to actions of the

fifth column stay-behinds, but there were also external activities that were to move the war to its next stage.

Moreover, the history also admits that in a secret directive by the North Vietnamese Politburo in May 1959, Hanoi ordered its Southern supporters to switch from political action to armed struggle. To provide help for the new fighting, Hanoi established a special task force, code named Group 559, which set up infiltration routes and moved "people, weapons and supplies" through Laos into South Vietnam.

When the N.L.F. was proclaimed in December 1960, this official Communist history goes on, it was done at the order of the party in Hanoi, and the Front's program "followed the line delineated by our party." These actions marked a critical turning point in the war, leading to the formation of bigger Viet Cong units and an increase in attacks on South Vietnamese Government posts. It was this stepped up activity that confronted President Kennedy and led him to increase the number of American advisors in South Vietnam.[18]

The NLF was the communist-front organization that was the political arm of the Vietcong and portrayed itself as the legitimate government of South Vietnam during the Vietnam War. "As a 'front' its aim was to bring together a disparate collection of elements opposed to Diem: various peasant, youth, religious, cultural, and other associations founded by the Vietminh during the war against the French; and remnants of the Cao Dai, Hoa Hao, and Binh Xuyen, which had retreated into their sanctuaries in the Mekong delta after their defeat by Diem five years earlier."[19] A description of the NLF described it as follows: "A broad yet communist-controlled coalition, the NLF is truly the Vietminh reborn."[20]

The previous quotes establish that infiltration from the North was occurring between 1959 and 1964, although it is said that the infiltration was mainly of the Vietminh that had been repatriated to the north in 1954. The implication to be drawn from this is that the infiltration was of indigenous Southern communists from the North. Hanoi did not admit until long after the war in Vietnam was over that there had been *any type* of infiltration from the North whatsoever. It was stated that by December 1960 "an estimated 4500 former South Vietnamese living in the North have infiltrated back to South Vietnam during the year."[21]

There will be more in-depth analysis of the nature of the NLF at another point in this book.

By the time the new U.S. president, John F. Kennedy, took office in January 1961 the situation in Vietnam had deteriorated significantly from the U.S. point of view. It continued to deteriorate through March 1961. "Citing that more than one-half of the rural region surrounding Saigon is under Communist control, and recalling the barely failed coup against Diem the preceding November, a national intelligence estimate prepared for President Kennedy declares that Diem and the Republic of Vietnam are facing an extremely critical period."[22]

John F. Kennedy, in his first attempt to rectify the deteriorating situation in Vietnam, approved sending 400 Special Forces and another 100 other military advisers to South Vietnam.

In June 1961 Kennedy met with Soviet premier Khrushchev in Vienna, with one of the results being that the situation in Vietnam was further placed into the cold war, containment, Truman Doctrine, domino theory, and SEATO context. "JFK returned from his meeting with Soviet Premier Nikita Khrushchev in Vienna in 1961 convinced that Communist 'Wars of National Liberation' would be the wave of the future. The local conflicts they support can turn in their favor through guerrillas or insurgents or subversion, JFK said. Kennedy also said: 'We have a problem in making our power credible, and Vietnam looks like the place.'"[23] U.S. attempts to overthrow Fidel Castro in Cuba in April 1961 with the Bay of Pigs fiasco had cast a shadow of doubt over Kennedy. There was some doubt as to the strength and resolve of this new, young president. Khrushchev (Kennedy and his advisers felt) was testing Kennedy's resolve at Vienna with his bellicose rhetoric. This combined with Khrushchev's previous statements concerning national wars of liberation caused Kennedy to feel that Vietnam was a testing place of the cold war and our cold war policies. Given this, it is no surprise that John Kennedy made the moves that began the escalation of U.S. involvement in Vietnam. Gen. William Westmoreland, the later commander of U.S. forces in Vietnam, said "And it was JFK who locked America into Vietnam until the bitter end."[24]

"When Kennedy took office in January 1961, there were some 900 advisors in Vietnam."[25] There were a great deal more by December 1961. "According to MAAG, US military forces have reached 3200."[26] MACV, the Military Assistance Command Vietnam, was established in February 1962 to control the military buildup that Kennedy had ordered. Referring to Kennedy it was said: "When he was assassinated in November 1963, that number had grown to about 16,300 U.S. military personnel, some of whom were engaged in active combat."[27] Officially, U.S. forces in Vietnam were there in an advisory capacity only in 1963.

Kennedy, as was mentioned before, further emphasized that Vietnam was a key part of the overall cold war. "To the New Frontier, Indochina represented *the* decisive battle that would determine whether guerrilla war could be stopped and the cold war won. Kennedy's interpretation of the conflict as a coordinated global conspiracy caused him to conclude that Southeast Asia was the place to restore his credibility after he had been browbeaten by Khrushchev at the Vienna Summit of June 1961."[28]

Soviet premier Nikita Khrushchev's statements about

support for wars of national liberation had the effect of allowing the United States to frame the Vietnam situation in the cold war context. It is well to remember that later Chinese pronouncements had the same effect on Pres. Lyndon Johnson: "In September 1965, the same misunderstanding would occur during the Johnson administration with respect to China, when Chinese Defense Minister Lin Piao's manifesto on 'People's War' spoke grandly of 'encircling' the world's industrial powers by revolutions throughout the Third World."[29]

Later it is believed that the Soviets' belligerent statements concerning wars of national liberation were tailored to deflect Chinese criticism of the Soviets' lack of revolutionary fervor more than to be a warning to the West. The Chinese statements for their part were somewhat misunderstood also: "The Johnson Administration interpreted this as a warning that China might intervene in Hanoi, ignoring Lin's subtext which stressed the need for self reliance among revolutionaries."[30] In diplomacy, perception might as well be reality. U.S. perception of Soviet and Chinese statements reinforced its notions of the cold war as an East–West struggle to be played out everywhere, including Vietnam.

During 1963, the situation continued to deteriorate in South Vietnam. As the United States increased its aid to the Diem regime, it also increased pressure on Diem to reform his government. It became increasingly apparent to the U.S. government that Diem seemed more interested in using the aid to develop an army to solidify his regime against internal opposition, such as the Buddhists and the sects, than to go after the communist threat. Diem's development of an army designed more to protect him from an internal coup than to destroy communists was reflected in the defeat his army suffered against the Vietcong at the Battle of Ap Bac in January of 1963. Ap Bac was a major defeat of a South Vietnamese unit at the hands of the Vietcong in what was one of the first major encounters between the two forces. U.S. reporters knew of the battle and reported on it negatively, receiving national attention in the United States: "Halberstram, Browne, and Sheehan wrote critical stories of the battle, quoting U.S. advisor Lieutenant John Paul Vann on the enemy's combat skill and the reluctance of the South Vietnamese troops to fight."[31]

U.S. policy makers increasingly began to believe that Diem was not the man to get the job done the way the United States wanted. Diem did not seem to be able to rally his troops against the Vietcong, and his persecution of other internal opposition, particularly the Buddhists, had gotten out of control as far as the Americans were concerned. Relations deteriorated between the United States and the Diem regime. Eventually, it was decided by the United States to give its tacit approval for the overthrow of Diem. Finally, a group of South Vietnamese generals overthrew and assassinated Diem on November 1, 1963. The overthrow of Diem had profound policy implications for the United States and its involvement in the Vietnam War:

By encouraging Diem's overthrow, America cast its involvement in Vietnam in concrete. Ultimately, every revolutionary war is about governmental legitimacy; undermining it is the guerrilla principal aim. Diem's overthrow handed that objective to Hanoi for free. As a consequence of Diem's feudal style of government, his removal affected every tier of civil administration down to the village level. Authority now had to be rebuilt from the ground up. And history teaches this iron law of revolutions: the more extensive the eradication of existing authority, the more its successors must rely on naked power to establish themselves. For, in the end, legitimacy involves the acceptance of authority without compulsion; its absence turns every contest into a test of strength. Prior to the coup, there had always existed, at least in theory, the possibility that America would refuse to become directly involved in military operations, much as

Eisenhower had done when he pulled back from the brink over Dien Bien Phu nearly a decade earlier. Since the coup had been justified to facilitate a more effective prosecution of the war, withdrawal disappeared as a policy option.[32]

The overthrow of Diem was obviously a turning point in U.S. policy. Not only had withdrawal been removed as an option, but also "because the Kennedy administration sanctioned the coup, Washington became morally and politically responsible for all the regimes that succeeded it."[33]

Diem was assassinated in early November of 1963 and Kennedy later in November of 1963. A new U.S. president, Lyndon B. Johnson, inherited a further deteriorating situation in Vietnam as the year 1964 approached. U.S. secretary of defense Robert McNamara summed up the situation as follows: "Secretary McNamara himself ruefully observed to President Johnson in December 1963: 'Vietcong progress has been great since the coup, with my best guess being that the situation has in fact been deteriorating since July.'"[34]

It had been a military coup led by Gen. Duong Van Minh that had overthrown the Diem regime in November 1963. The ruling military junta that Minh and the other generals established proved to be inept as political rulers. They were overthrown in January 1964 by Maj. Gen. Nguyen Kanh. "American officials soon learned that coups seemed to generate coups: Throughout 1964 and 1965, weak South Vietnamese regimes succeeded each other, until the relatively durable team of Nguyen Cao Ky and Nguyen Van Thieu assumed power in June of 1965."[35]

Exploiting the internal chaos in South Vietnam, the communists at the behest of North Vietnam began to move the war in Vietnam to a new level. "The power brokers in Hanoi grasped their opportunity immediately. A Communist Party Central Committee meeting in December 1963 laid down the new strategy: guerrilla units would be strengthened, and infiltration into the South accelerated. Most important, North Vietnamese regular units would be introduced . . . Soon thereafter, the 325th North Vietnamese regular division began moving into the South."[36]

Communist power in South Vietnam, as is recalled, began with Vietminh stay-behinds who did not go north in 1954, reinforced by return of former Vietminh who had gone north, coming back south after 1959, and by 1964 further reinforcement and strengthening with *North Vietnamese regulars*. It should be noted that at this time U.S. troop strength in Vietnam was at about sixteen thousand and they were still in an advisory capacity.

By late 1963 and early 1964 U.S. policy in Vietnam was at a crossroad. "On December 21, 1963, McNamara reported to the new President that the security situation in South Vietnam had become very disturbing. America could no longer avoid facing the choice which had been implicit all along: dramatic escalation of military involvement or the collapse of South Vietnam."[37]

Allowing the collapse of South Vietnam in 1964 or 1965 would have been contrary to the logic of U.S. post–World War II foreign policy development. The Truman Doctrine and its evolution in the policy of containment had caused us to place the struggle in Vietnam in the context of containment. Soviet and Chinese pronouncements along with North Vietnamese actions reinforced U.S. perceptions, whether the perceptions were correct or incorrect. The SEATO agreement was put into place as a result of the previous logic and our belief that the fall of South Vietnam would be the important domino falling, therefore fulfilling our fear embodied in the domino theory. The deck seemed stacked in the direction of escalation in reference to the Vietnam conflict. This was the logical outcome of the evolution of these post–World War II policies.

Before the United States escalated further there would be one more linchpin that finalized escalation and a U.S. combat role. This event was the Gulf of Tonkin Incident and the resulting Gulf of Tonkin Resolution, which will be covered in the next chapter.

The way it stood for Lyndon Johnson in 1964 could be summarized as follows: "If indeed Kennedy had felt the sting of realization that America had embarked on an unsustainable course, he needed to reverse only his own course; Johnson on the other hand would have had to jettison the apparent policy of a revered, fallen predecessor."[38]

Lyndon Johnson's own views, however, lent themselves to the mind-set of escalation also. "The new President, Lyndon Baines Johnson, interpreted intervention by North Vietnamese units as a classic case of overt aggression."[39]

Notes

1. William Appleman Williams, Thomas McCormick, Lloyd Gardner, Walter LeFeber, *America in Vietnam, a Documentary History* (New York: Anchor Press/Doubleday, 1985), p. 140.
2. Neil Sheehan, *A Bright Shining Lie, John Paul Vann and America in Vietnam* (New York: Random House, 1988), p. 184.
3. Jack C. Plano and Milton Greenberg, *The American Political Dictionary* (Orlando, FL: Holt, Rhinehart, and Winston, 1989), p. 507.
4. Williams et al., *America in Vietnam,* p. 48.
5. Tony Murdoch, Joan M. Crouse, and Pam O'Connell, *Vietnam* (White Plains, NY: Longman, 1994), p. 50.
6. John Foster Dulles, from a speech delivered to the Overseas Press Club of America, New York, March 29, 1954, reprinted in David L. Bender, *The Vietnam War, Opposing Viewpoints* (St. Paul, MN: Greenhaven, 1984), p. 19.
7. Murdoch, Crouse, and O'Connell, *Vietnam,* p. 50.
8. Henry Kissinger, *Diplomacy* (New York: Simon and Schuster, 1994), p. 635.
9. Ibid., p. 636.
10. "United States Objectives and Courses of Action with Respect to

Southeast Asia," Statement of Policy by the National Security Council, 1952, in ibid., pp. 626–27.
11. United States Government, *Public Papers of the Presidents of the United States: Dwight D. Eisenhower, 1954* (Washington, DC: 1958), pp. 381–90 in Williams et al., *America in Vietnam,* pp.156–57.
12. Plano and Greenberg, *The American Political Dictionary,* p. 482.
13. Norman Podhoretz, *Why We Were in Vietnam* (New York: Simon and Schuster, 1982), p. 66.
14. Ibid., p. 41.
15. Ibid.
16. Harry G. Summers, Jr., *Vietnam War Almanac* (New York: Facts on File, 1985), p. 65.
17. Ibid., p. 352.
18. Fox Butterfield, quoting George Mct. Kahin and John W. Lewis, *The United States in Vietnam,* in "The New Vietnam Scholarship," *New York Times Magazine,* February 13, 1983, p. 32.
19. Stanley Karnow, *Vietnam: A History* (New York: Viking, 1983), pp. 238–39.
20. John S. Bowman, ed., *The Vietnam War: An Almanac* (New York: World Almanac, 1985), p. 50.
21. Ibid.
22. Ibid.
23. Harry G. Summers, in an editorial in *Vietnam Magazine,* June, 1992, p. 6.
24. Ibid., quoting William Westmoreland from *Perspectives,* February 1990.
25. Summers, *Vietnam Magazine,* p. 6.
26. Bowman, *The Vietnam War,* p. 54.
27. Summers, *Vietnam Magazine,* p. 6.
28. Kissinger, *Diplomacy,* p. 645.
29. Ibid., p. 644.
30. Ibid., p. 645.
31. Summers, *Vietnam Magazine,* p. 184.
32. Kissinger, *Diplomacy,* p. 655.
33. Butterfield, quoting Larry Bremen, *Planning a Tragedy: The Americanization of the War,* in "The New Vietnam Scholarship," p. 45.
34. "Untold Story of the Road to War in Vietnam," *U.S. News and World Report,* October 10, 1983, p. 16.
35. Ibid., p. 24.
36. Kissinger, *Diplomacy,* p. 656.
37. Ibid.
38. Ibid., p. 657.
39. Ibid., p. 656.

3

The Gulf of Tonkin Resolution

Nineteen sixty-four was a year that witnessed decline and set-backs for U.S. aspirations in South Vietnam. It was a year of military juntas, coups, and general political instability for the South Vietnamese government. Meanwhile, the NLF and the communists in Hanoi viewed it as an opportune time to make substantial gains in their effort to destroy the government of South Vietnam:

> Determined to attain the goal that had eluded them in 1954, the North Vietnamese leaders increasingly recognized that they could not succeed without a major commitment of their own resources. At the Central Committee's Ninth Plenum in December 1963, the party leadership decided to instruct the Vietcong to step up its political agitation and military opera-tions against the South Vietnamese government. More impor-tant, Hanoi decided to expand infiltration into the south and even to send its own regular units into the war. [1]

To conclude that the United States shaped its policy with-out deep thinking and discussion would be a grave error. Study after study, report after report, and experts on top of experts pondered the course of action the United States should pursue to create stability in South Vietnam and prevent a communist takeover. The large shadow over this thinking remained our fear that allowing South Vietnam to fall to communism would be a crack in the wall of containment. The policy makers of the day were shaped by the lessons of appeasement in Munich in 1938, the fall of Eastern Europe to the Soviets, and the fall of China to communism in 1949.

The overriding position of most of the experts was that the United States must do what was necessary to prevent a communist takeover of South Vietnam. How to accomplish this became the question. Should the United States begin a bombing campaign against North Vietnam? Should it bring in active combat troops to change its advisory role? For the most part the answer to these questions in 1964 was no. The United States basically would continue the same role it had in 1963: providing military and economic assistance to the South Vietnamese regime while remaining in an essentially advisory capacity. In addition, the United States approved some covert operations that are more far-reaching and will be dealt with later in this chapter.

Long-range thinking, however, understood well that there might be U.S. escalation and more direct involvement in the future, and certain items were being fashioned by mid-1964 that would facilitate these potentialities. These activities and events culminated in the Gulf of Tonkin Resolution in August of 1964. The Gulf of Tonkin Resolution was the closest thing to a declaration of war that the United States had in reference to the Vietnam War. It also became the legalistic, constitutional basis for U.S. pursuit of the Vietnam War. In short, it was the last element of foreign policy doctrine that combined with the other previously mentioned doctrines that evolved into U.S. pursuit of the Vietnam War.

In May 1964 the CIA had submitted a gloomy report of a deteriorating situation in South Vietnam. Aware that more direct action might be necessary, the president asked the Defense and State Departments to prepare an "integrated political-military plan for graduated action against North Vietnam." "In conjunction with this planning, the State Department drafted a resolution seeking congressional validation of expanded U.S. military action in Indochina."[2]

Pres. Lyndon Johnson wanted to avoid what he considered a mistake by Pres. Harry S Truman when Truman failed to enlist congressional support for military action in Korea.

> This was the origin of what would become the Tonkin Gulf Resolution. It reflected President Johnson's oft-repeated warning that, if events ever forced us to expand the war, we must avoid the mistake President Truman had made in Korea, i.e., engaging in military operations without congressional approval. Congress will not accept any responsibility for a "crash landing" unless it has also been in on the "takeoff," said Johnson, and therefore he was determined to have congressional authorization of any major U.S. military action in Southeast Asia if he ever had to initiate it.[3]

Strategy in Vietnam in the six months preceding the Gulf of Tonkin Resolution included Operation Plan 34A (OPLAN 34A or just 34A). This covert operation was much more of an attempt to bring the war to North Vietnam than had occurred previously. It also tied into the Gulf of Tonkin Incident, which then translated itself into the Gulf of Tonkin Resolution. OPLAN 34A was an attempt to stop the communist insurgency in South Vietnam and was backed by Defense Secretary Robert McNamara. "According to Robert McNamara its goal was that the 'progressively escalating pressure from the clandestine attacks might eventually force Hanoi to order Vietcong guerrillas in Vietnam and the Pathet Lao in Laos to halt their insurrections.'"[4] "Plan 34A comprised two types of operations: in one, boats and aircraft dropped South Vietnamese agents equipped with radios into North Vietnam to conduct sabotage and to gather intelligence; in the other, high-speed patrol boats manned by South Vietnamese or foreign mercenary crews launched hit-and-run attacks against North Vietnamese shore and island installations."[5]

A best-case scenario hoped that this operation would convince the North to cease aiding the Vietcong, and a worst-case scenario viewed this as a cheap way to harass the North as a form of retaliation for the North's aid to the Vietcong. In reality the raids accomplished very little of value in the pursuit of the war.

Another type of operation was occurring in the Tonkin Gulf region simultaneously; these were known as DESOTO patrols. While occurring separately, these patrols became involved in the Gulf of Tonkin Incident, which led to the Gulf of Tonkin Resolution.

> DESOTO patrols differed substantially in purpose and procedure from 34A operations. They were part of a system of global electronic reconnaissance carried out by specially equipped U.S. naval vessels. Operating in international waters, these vessels collected radio and radar signals emanating from shore-based stations on the periphery of Communist countries such as the Soviet Union, China, North Korea, and, more to the point here, North Vietnam. These patrols resembled those of Soviet trawlers off our coasts. The information collected could be used in the event U.S. military operations ever became necessary against these countries. . . . Although some individuals knew of both 34A operations and DESOTO patrols, the approval process for each was compartmentalized, and few, if any, senior officials either planned or followed in detail the operational schedules of both.[6]

In late July and early August of 1964 the events unfolded that were to become known as the Gulf of Tonkin Incident and the Gulf of Tonkin Resolution. As the reader should know by now, these events were pivotal in reference to United States' involvement in the Vietnam War. The following will attempt to relate to the reader the actual events that played out during this time. At this point the account is simply a narrative of what happened. There are many conflicts in the interpretation of what actually did and did not occur. Best evidence, however, indicates that the U.S. Navy came under attack.

At about midnight July 30, 1964, six "swifts," the special PT boats used by the South Vietnamese for their covert raids, attacked two islands in the Gulf of Tonkin, Hon Me and Hon Ngu. The commandos were unable to land on the islands but fired on island installations. The U.S. destroyer *Maddox*, which was a DESOTO mission ship, monitored radar and radio transmissions from its position 120 miles away.

By August 2 the *Maddox* was cruising around the Tonkin Gulf further monitoring the radio and radar signals following the attack by the South Vietnamese. U.S. crews intercepted one North Vietnamese message as indicating they were preparing "military operations," which the *Maddox*'s captain, John Herrick, assumed meant some retaliatory attack. He was instructed by his superiors to remain in the area. Early in the afternoon, three North Vietnamese patrol boats began to chase the *Maddox*. At about 3:00 P.M., Captain Herrick ordered his crew to commence firing as the craft came within 10,000 yards, and he radioed the U.S. aircraft carrier *Ticonderoga* for air support. The North Vietnamese boats each fired one torpedo at the *Maddox,* but two missed and the third failed to explode. U.S. gunfire hit one of the craft, and then three U.S. Crusader jets proceeded to strafe them. After about twenty minutes, *Maddox* gunners had sunk one of the boats and the other two were crippled. Only one bullet hit the *Maddox,* and there were no U.S. casualties.[7] "At the time of the incident, the *Maddox* lay in international waters, more than twenty-five miles off the North Vietnamese coast."[8]

At 11:30 A.M. on August 2, the president met with his senior advisers to study the latest reports and consider a U.S. response. . . . The group believed that it was possible that a local North Vietnamese commander—rather than a senior official—had taken the initiative, and the president therefore decided not to retaliate. He agreed instead to send a stiff protest note to Hanoi and to continue the patrol, adding another destroyer, the *C. Turner Joy*.[9]

At about eight o'clock in the evening on August 4, the *Maddox* intercepted radio messages from the North Vietnamese that gave Captain Herrick the impression that their patrol boats were planning an attack, Herrick called for air support from the *Ticonderoga* again, and eight Crusader jets soon appeared overhead. In the darkness, neither the pilots nor the ship crews could see any enemy craft, but about ten o'clock the sonar operators were reporting torpedoes approaching; the U.S. destroyers maneuvered to avoid the torpedoes and began to fire. When the action ended about two hours later, U.S. officers reported sinking two, possibly three, North Vietnamese craft. In fact, no American will be sure of ever having seen any enemy boats or any enemy gunfire.[10]

Questions of the validity of reports of a second attack have been bantered about in the years since the incidents. The issue, in reality, is moot because the second attack was *perceived* in Washington to have occurred. This perception was formed from the best information available at the time. Defense Secretary Robert McNamara relates his communications with Cyrus Vance and Admiral Sharp, commander of U.S. naval forces in the Pacific. McNamara had requested that air force lieutenant general David A. Burchinal call Admiral Sharp in Honolulu several times to obtain details of the incident. Information obtained was reviewed at a meeting with the Joint Chiefs of Staff.

At 4:47 P.M., Cy and I met with the chiefs to review the evidence relating to the alleged second attack. Five factors in particular persuaded us it had occurred: the *Turner Joy* had been illuminated when fired upon by automatic weapons; one of the destroyers had observed PT boat cockpit lights; antiaircraft batteries had fired on two U.S. aircraft overflying the area; we had intercepted and decoded a North Vietnamese message indicating two of its boats had been sunk; and Admiral Sharp called Burchinal and said no doubt now existed that an attack on the destroyers had been carried out.[11]

By 11:00 A.M. on August 4, President Johnson was informed and the Joint Chiefs of Staff had begun to select targets for reprisal air strikes (from a list drawn up by the end of May). At a meeting of the National Security Council about noon, McNamara, Rusk, and McGeorge Bundy recommended such reprisal strikes to the president. Johnson was more cautious, but at a second session of the NSC that afternoon he ordered that reprisal strikes be made. At 6:45 P.M. President Johnson met with sixteen leaders from both parties in Congress to inform them of the second unprovoked attack, the imminent reprisal strikes, and his intention to ask for a congressional resolution. At 11:30 P.M. President Johnson appeared on national television and announced that the reprisal strikes were under way because of the unprovoked attack on U.S. ships. The president assured the world that "we still seek no wider war."[12]

On August 5, F-8 Crusaders, A-1 Skyhawks, and A-4 Skyhawks, flying from the carriers USS *Ticonderoga* and *Constellation,* flew sixty-four sorties over a 100-mile area of North Vietnam along the Gulf of Tonkin. They destroyed or damaged an estimated twenty-five North Vietnamese PT boats (claimed by the United States to comprise about one-half of the North Vietnamese navy). Bases at Hongay, Loc Ghao, Phuc Loi, and Quang Khe were attacked. At Phuc Loi an oil storage depot was destroyed, which was estimated to be about 10 percent of North Vietnam's oil storage facilities. Raiders also destroyed seven antiaircraft installations at Vinh.[13]

Two U.S. planes were damaged and two others were shot down by North Vietnamese antiaircraft fire. A U.S. pilot, Everett Alvarez, was shot down and remained a prisoner of war until the cease-fire was reached in 1973.

After the Gulf of Tonkin Incident occurred, things were put in motion to send a resolution to Congress, drafted back in May, that would give congressional validation for expanding military operations in Indochina. This Gulf of Tonkin Resolution was presented by William Bundy to the two congressional leaders who were to sponsor its passage on August 5. These leaders were Democratic senator J. William Fullbright of Arkansas, who was chairman of the Senate Foreign Relations Committee, and Democratic representative Thomas E. Morgan of Pennsylvania, who was chairman of the House Foreign Affairs Committee. The next day Defense Secretary Robert McNamara and Secretary of State Dean Rusk appeared before a joint congressional committee on foreign affairs and presented the Johnson administration's arguments for the resolution.

The resolution went before the Full House and Senate on August 7, 1964. Both Houses overwhelmingly approved of Public Law 88-408, which became known as the Gulf of Tonkin Resolution. The vote was 82–2 in the Senate, where only Sen. Wayne Morse, Democrat of Oregon, and Sen. Ernest Gruening, Democrat of Alaska, voted against it. In the House of Representatives the vote was 416 for and 0 against the resolution. The text of the resolution follows:

The Resolution: Whereas naval units of the Communist regime in Vietnam, in violation of the principles of the Charter of the United Nations and of international law, have deliberately and repeatedly attacked United States naval vessels lawfully present in international waters, and have thereby created a serious threat to international peace;

Whereas these attacks are part of a deliberate and systematic campaign of aggression that the Communist regime in North Vietnam has been waging against its neighbors and the nations joined with them in the collective defense of their freedom;

Whereas the United States is assisting the peoples of southeast Asia to protect their freedom and has no territorial, military or political ambitions in that area, but desires only that these peoples should be left in peace to work out their own destinies in their own way: now, therefore, be it

Resolved by the Senate and House of Representatives of the United States of America in Congress assembled, That the Congress approves and supports the determination of the President, as Commander in Chief, to take all necessary measures to repel any armed attack against the forces of the United States and to prevent further aggression.

Sec. 2. The United States regards as vital to its national interest and to world peace the maintenance of international peace and security to southeast Asia. Consonant with the Constitution and the Charter of the United Nations and in accordance with its obligations under the Southeast Asia Collective Defense Treaty, the United States is, therefore, prepared, as the President determines, to take all necessary steps, including the use of armed force, to assist any member or protocol state of the Southeast Asia Collective Defense Treaty requesting assistance in defense of its freedom.

Sec. 3. This resolution shall expire when the President shall determine that the peace and security of the area is reasonably assured by international conditions created by action of the United Nations or otherwise, except that it may be terminated earlier by concurrent resolution of the Congress.[14]

This resolution culminates the framework of U.S. foreign

policy doctrines and actions that led to U.S. involvement in the Vietnam War. The policy of containment, the Truman Doctrine, the Domino Theory, and the SEATO Treaty (which is mentioned in the resolution itself) are all tied together and made ready to implement once the Gulf of Tonkin Resolution is in place. The president of the United States, with this resolution, was given very broad powers to make a determination of what he perceived to be communist aggression and a threat to containment and Western interests. North Vietnamese actions and the actions of the NLF in South Vietnam were viewed as an extension of international monolithic communism. These actions conflicted with our stated foreign policy doctrines. It did not happen immediately, but Pres. Lyndon Johnson within a year responded to violations of our foreign policy doctrines and used his power under the Gulf of Tonkin Resolution to commit U.S. troops into combat in what became the longest war in U.S. history.

The resolution became controversial as the war continued. There have been accusations of duplicity and manufacturing of the incident as an excuse to expand the war.

> It is true that the president seized upon the incident in order to approve and carry out measures that had been recommended to him earlier, but this does not establish that the attack was deliberately provoked, let alone that it rests on a fabrication. While the sonar and radar readings and the visual sightings of torpedoes can be questioned as unreliable and inconclusive, there is other unambiguous evidence which leaves no doubt of the fact of an attack.[15]

Some statements that apply to the resolution should be mentioned at this point:

> The language of the resolution plainly granted the powers the president subsequently used, and Congress understood the

breadth of those powers when it overwhelmingly approved the resolution on August 7, 1964. But no doubt exists that Congress did *not* intend to authorize without further, full consultation the expansion of U.S. forces in Vietnam from 16,000 to 500,000 men, initiating large-scale combat operations with the risk of an expanded war with China and the Soviet Union, and extending U.S. involvement in Vietnam for many years to come.[16]

The views of Pres. Lyndon Johnson were expressed in a different manner as U.S. military involvement increased.

Decisions were deferred as we groped for the least bad road to follow. While the debate raged, reporters pressed Johnson about recent Senate requests for further congressional action—going beyond the Tonkin Gulf Resolution—before he deployed more U.S. troops. He deflected the questioners by saying, "Anybody [who] has read the resolution" could see it authorized the president "to take all—all—all necessary measures" he thought necessary in the situation.[17]

"It was not until August 18, 1967, three years after it had been enacted, that President Lyndon B. Johnson repudiated the Gulf of Tonkin resolution as the legal basis for the war and fell back on the authority granted him by Article II of the Constitution as commander in chief of the armed forces."[18]

On March 1, 1966, an amendment to repeal the resolution was defeated in the Senate 95 to 5. The resolution was finally terminated by Congress in May 1970, but the Vietnam War continued for three more years. An obvious legacy of the Gulf of Tonkin Resolution was the War Powers Act of 1973, which placed limits and restrictions of executive powers to commit U.S. troops to combat in foreign nations.

The policy of containment, the Truman Doctrine, the Domino Theory, SEATO, and the Gulf of Tonkin Resolution were the philosophical and quasi-legal underpinnings of our involvement in the Vietnam War. With this background, this book, in the remainder of part 1, will explore the details that moved us from philosophy in 1964 to commitment in 1965 and then briefly overview the major events during the course of the war.

Notes

1. George C. Herring, *America's Longest War, the United States and Vietnam 1950–1975* (New York: McGraw Hill, 1986), p. 110.
2. Robert S. McNamara, *In Retrospect, the Tragedy and Lessons of Vietnam* (New York: Random House, 1995), p. 120.
3. Ibid.
4. Tony Murdoch, Joan M. Crouse, and Pam O'Connell, *Vietnam* (White Plains, NY: Longman, 1994), p. 92.
5. McNamara, *In Retrospect,* p. 129.
6. Ibid., p. 130.
7. John S. Bowman, ed., *The Vietnam War: An Almanac* (New York: World Almanac, 1985), p. 82.
8. McNamara, *In Retrospect,* p. 131.
9. Ibid.
10. Bowman, *The Vietnam War,* p. 84.
11. McNamara, *In Retrospect,* p. 134.
12. Bowman, *The Vietnam War,* p. 84.
13. Ibid.
14. *Congressional Record,* August 5–7, 1964, pp. 18132–33, 18406–7, 18458–59, 18470–71.
15. Guenter Lewy, *America in Vietnam* (New York: Oxford University Press, 1978), p. 35.
16. McNamara, *In Retrospect,* p. 142.
17. President's News Conference, June 17, 1965, *Public Papers, Lyndon B. Johnson, 1965,* bk. 2, pp. 669–85, as cited in ibid., p. 191.
18. Harry G. Summers, *Vietnam* (August 1994), p. 4.

4

America's War

In the fall of 1964 massive political instability plagued the government of South Vietnam. Coup after coup continued to change the leadership at the top. None of these incompetent governments had any names worth remembering, nor were any of the succession of regimes able to develop efficient administration of the country. Meanwhile Vietcong control of territory and population continued to increase and the possibility of the total collapse of the South Vietnamese government became a distinct possibility.

The U.S. position at this time was to continue to support the South Vietnamese government the way we had previously:

> President Johnson's public posture during this period, which coincided with the presidential election, reflected his hesitation to be drawn into a wider war. American boys, he stated several times, should not be sent to Asia to do the fighting which Asian boys, with American advice and equipment, should be doing for themselves. "That is the course we are following. So we are not going north and drop bombs at this stage of the game, and we are not going south and run out and leave it for the Communists to take over."[1]

During the latter half of 1964 American foreign policy tried to balance two objectives in Vietnam. These were to avoid the introduction of American combat forces while simultaneously preventing South Vietnam from falling under communist control.

> To do so became increasingly difficult. Meanwhile, conditions in South Vietnam, particularly in the political realm, worsened steadily, and in the face of what seemed like the Saigon government's imminent collapse, we remained deeply divided—over what to do. We held meeting after meeting and exchanged memo after memo. We thrashed about, frustrated by Vietnam's complexity and our own differences and confusion. But we still failed to achieve consensus or solve the problem.[2]

Near the end of November some proposals were being seriously considered. Strategies for using U.S. air power against North Vietnam were put forth by senior advisers. "It was to be a two-phase operation, with the first part confined to reprisal raids against the North and limited bombing raids against infiltration tracks in Laos. Known as Barrel Roll, the operation was to last about a month."[3] President Johnson approved this phase by December 1. "The second phase was to be a lengthier offensive, lasting between two and six months and targeting key areas in North Vietnam."[4] Johnson did not make this commitment at this time, but the bombing plans were put on the back burner.

By late January 1965, after months of indecision and uncertainty, National Security Adviser McGeorge Bundy and Defense Secretary Robert McNamara gave President Johnson a memo later referred as the "fork-in the road" memo. Excerpts follow:

> Both of us are now pretty well convinced that our current policy can lead only to disastrous defeat. What we are doing now, essentially, is to wait and hope for a stable government. Our December directives make it very plain that wider action against the communists will not take place unless we can get such a

government. In the last six weeks that effort has been unsuccessful, and Bob and I are persuaded that there is no real hope
of success in this area unless and until our own policy and priorities change. . . . The Vietnamese know just as well as we do
that the Viet Cong are gaining in the countryside. Meanwhile,
they see the enormous power of the United States withheld,
and they get little sense of firm and active U.S. policy. They feel
that we are unwilling to take serious risks. . . . The basic directive says that we will not go further until there is a stable government, and no one has much hope that there is going to be a
stable government while we sit still. The result is that we are
pinned into a policy of first aid for squabbling politicos and passive reaction to events we do not try to control. Or it seems.

Bob and I believe that the worst course of action is to continue in this essentially passive role which can only lead to
eventual defeat and an invitation to get out in humiliating circumstances.

We see two alternatives. The *first* is to use our military
power in the Far East and to force a change in Communist policy. The *second* is to deploy all our resources along a track of
negotiation, aimed at salvaging what little can be preserved
with no major addition to our present military risks. Bob and I
tend to favor the first course, but we believe that both should
be carefully studied and that alternative programs should be
argued out before you.[5]

There is absolutely no doubt at this point U.S. foreign policy was at a fork in the road, or a crossroad. The South Vietnamese regime(s) was (were) unstable, with no foreseeable
change in this status. It had been our number-one priority to
have a stable regime to stave off a communist takeover. The
United States was beginning to conclude that the only way a
stable regime would exist in the South was if we took much
stronger military action against the Viet Cong and the North
Vietnamese. The United States increasingly felt that if it pur-
sued its present course South Vietnam would fall to the com-

57

munists. One alternative would have been to cut U.S. losses and exit. The other alternative was to escalate U.S. military effort. The United States *was* at a critical juncture in early 1965!

Although a formal decision had not been made, it became increasingly the consensus of the Johnson administration that they would act in response to the next communist challenge with a gradual beginning of full-scale bombing of North Vietnam. They did not have to wait very long. On February 6, 1965, a U.S. Army barracks at Pleiku and a nearby helicopter base were attacked. The raid killed nine Americans. Within hours President Johnson ordered Operation Flaming Dart, a series of strikes against targets already drawn up by military planners.[6] "Four days later another U.S. building was attacked, and Johnson responded with more air strikes. On February 24 Operation Rolling Thunder was put into action on the pretext that retaliation against the North was required. This was no tit-for-tat counterstrike but, rather, the beginning of regular bombing raids."[7] Rolling Thunder originally was designed to interdict North Vietnamese infiltration routes in southern North Vietnam. Later it was expanded to include North Vietnamese ammunition dumps and oil storage facilities. By the spring of 1967 it was further expanded to include power plants, factories, and airfields in the Hanoi-Haiphong area. The operation was ended in November 1968.

It has been posited that this U.S. escalation was responded to by escalation by the North Vietnamese. It appears, however, that U.S. policy makers had been aware of North Vietnamese escalation for some time. One regiment had departed from the North in September or October of 1964. This regiment was followed by another in October and yet another in December. The North had a minimum of 5,000 men in the South by March 1965.[8] "The initial escalation, through the introduction of North Vietnamese combat forces, thus was carried out by the Communists, well before the American decision to bomb North Vietnam."[9]

The time period of January 28–July 28, 1965, was the beginning of massive escalation. During this period total U.S. troop strength was raised from 23,000 to 175,000, and it was assumed that there would be more troops needed in the future. U.S. ground forces evolved into a combat role during this time period. This development will be traced shortly.

In February, the State Department issued a White Paper on Vietnam that summarized American views on the situation in Vietnam at that time. It follows:

> South Vietnam is fighting for its life against a brutal campaign of terror and armed attack inspired, directed, supplied, and controlled by the Communist regime in Hanoi. This flagrant aggression has been going on for years, but recently the pace has quickened and the threat has now become acute.
>
> The war in Vietnam is a new kind of war, a fact as yet poorly understood in most parts of the world. Much of the confusion that prevails in the thinking of many people, and even governments, stems from this basic misunderstanding. For in Vietnam a totally new brand of aggression has been loosed against an independent people who want to make their way in peace and freedom. Vietnam is not another Greece, where indigenous guerrilla forces used friendly neighboring territory as a sanctuary.
>
> Vietnam is not another Malaya, where Communist guerrillas were, for the most part, physically distinguishable from the peaceful majority they sought to control.
>
> Vietnam is not another Philippines, where Communist guerrillas were physically separated from the source of their moral and physical support.
>
> Above all, the war in Vietnam is not a spontaneous and local rebellion against the established government.
>
> There are elements in the Communist program of conquest directed against South Vietnam common to each of the

previous areas of aggression and subversion. But there is one fundamental difference. In Vietnam a Communist government has set out deliberately to conquer a sovereign people in a neighboring state. And to achieve its end, it has used every resource of its own government to carry out its carefully planned program of concealed aggression. North Vietnam's commitment to seize control of the South is no less total than was the commitment of the regime in North Korea in 1950. But knowing the consequences of the latter's undisguised attack, the planners in Hanoi have tried desperately to conceal their hand. They have failed and their aggression is as real as that of an invading army.

This report is a summary of the massive evidence of North Vietnamese aggression obtained by the Government of South Vietnam. This evidence has been jointly analyzed by South Vietnamese and American experts. The evidence shows that the hard core of the Communist forces attacking South Vietnam were trained in the North and ordered into the South by Hanoi. It shows that the key leadership of the Vietcong (VC), the officers and much of the cadre, many of the technicians, political organizers, and propagandists have come from the North and operate under Hanoi's direction. It shows that the training of essential military personnel and their infiltration into the South is directed by the Military High Command in Hanoi. In recent months new types of weapons have been introduced in the VC army, for which all ammunition must come from outside sources. Communist China and other Communist states have been the prime suppliers of these weapons and ammunition, and they have been channeled primarily through North Vietnam.

The directing force behind the effort to conquer South Vietnam is the Communist Party in the North, the Lap Dong (Workers) Party. As in every Communist state, the party is an integral part of the regime itself. North Vietnamese officials have expressed their firm determination to absorb South Vietnam into the Communist world.

Through its Central Committee, which controls the Government of the North, the Lao Dong Party directs the total political and military effort of the Vietcong. The Military High Command in the North trains the military men and sends them into South Vietnam. The Central Research Agency, North Vietnam's central intelligence organization, directs the elaborate espionage and subversion effort . . .

Under Hanoi's overall direction the Communists have established an extensive machine for carrying on the war within South Vietnam. The focal point is the Central Office for South Vietnam with its political and military subsections and other specialized agencies. A subordinate part of this Central Office is the Liberation Front for South Vietnam. The front was formed at Hanoi's order in 1960. Its principal function is to influence opinion abroad and to create the false impression that aggression in South Vietnam is an indigenous rebellion against the established Government.

For more than 10 years the people and the Government of South Vietnam, exercising the inherent right of self-defense, have fought back against these efforts to extend Communist power south across the 17th parallel. The United States has responded to the appeals of the Government of the Republic of Vietnam for help in this defense of the freedom and independence of its land and its people.

In 1961 the Department of State issued a report called A Threat to the Peace. It described North Vietnam's program to seize South Vietnam. The evidence in that report had been presented by the Government of the Republic of Vietnam to the International Control Commission (ICC). A special report by the ICC in June 1962 upheld the validity of that evidence. The Commission held that there was "sufficient evidence to show beyond reasonable doubt" that North Vietnam had sent arms and men into South Vietnam to carry out subversion with the aim of overthrowing the legal Government there. The ICC found the authorities in Hanoi in specific violation of four provisions of the Geneva Accords of 1954.

Since then, new and even more impressive evidence of Hanoi's aggression has accumulated. The Government of the

United States believes that evidence should be presented to its own citizens and to the world. It is important for free men to know what has been happening in Vietnam, and how, and why. That is the purpose of this report . . .

The record is conclusive. It establishes beyond question that North Vietnam is carrying out a careful conceived plan of aggression against the South. It shows that North Vietnam has intensified its efforts in the years since it was condemned by the International Control Commission. It proves that Hanoi continues to press its systematic program of armed aggression into South Vietnam. This aggression violates the United Nations Charter. It is directly contrary to the Geneva Accords of 1954 and of 1962 to which North Vietnam is a party. It is a fundamental threat to the freedom and security of South Vietnam.

The people of South Vietnam have chosen to resist this threat. At their request, the United States has taken its place beside them in their defensive struggle. The United States seeks no territory, no military bases, no favored position. But we have learned the meaning of aggression elsewhere in the post-war world, and we have met it.

If peace can be restored in South Vietnam, the United States will be ready at once to reduce its military involvement. But it will not abandon friends who want to remain free. It will do what must be done to help them. The choice now between peace and continued and increasingly destructive conflict is one for the authorities in Hanoi to make. [10]

A few key concepts concerning U.S. policy come through very strongly in this paper. The United States believed the struggle in South Vietnam was not a home-grown uprising but more akin to an invasion from the North. The legitimate government of South Vietnam asked for the assistance of the United States. Also, the United States reiterated that it would do what was necessary to protect the freedom of the South. The rationale for military escalation had been put in place. U.S. strategy of taking the war to the North, it was hoped, would convince the North of the futility of its effort to overthrow the South Vietnamese government. The goal throughout the war was the same: stop the South Vietnamese government from crumbling, prove to the North and Viet Cong that a military victory was impossible, and get the parties to the bargaining table for an acceptable settlement.

"Wars generate their own momentum and follow the law of unanticipated consequences. Vietnam proved to be no exception. President Johnson's authorization of Operation Rolling Thunder not only started the air war but unexpectedly triggered the introduction of U.S. troops into ground combat as well."[11] At first more troops were needed to protect the air bases where the bombing raids originated. That was followed by an enclave strategy and the necessity of more troops. Ultimately, full-scale aggressive combat operations were authorized and larger and larger numbers of combat troops were necessary.

On March 8, 1965, two U.S. Marine battalions landed at Danang to provide base security for U.S. air bases. It was anticipated that there possibly would be Vietcong attacks on the bases. The decision to bomb had led logically to the introduction of these first combat troops.

It became clear after six weeks of Rolling Thunder that the North was not going to have its will bent easily. Once the United States realized that bombing alone would not break the enemy's will a decision was made to deploy 40,000 more combat troops to implement an enclave strategy. The enclaves were primarily fifty-mile defensive zones around bases. The troops, however, were not strictly limited to a defensive role. In early April the president had "agreed to change the marines' mission from base security to active combat."[12]

The march to war continued through May 1965 into June and July. During this time period the South Vietnamese army continued to lose ground and was on the verge of total disintegration. General Westmoreland, the commander of U.S. forces, had his grave doubts about the South's ability and willingness to keep fighting confirmed by events of this period. He concluded that more U.S. forces were needed. With the support of the Joint Chiefs of Staff he requested another 150,000 troops and an end to the enclave strategy. Westmoreland felt that the time had come to move fully onto the offensive.[13]

In late July the decisions were made that plotted the course for the next seven years of fighting in Vietnam. President Johnson did not approve an all-out bombing campaign of the North as most military advisers advocated but did permit a gradual intensification of the bombing of the North.

> At the same time, the President approved a major new commitment of ground forces and a new strategy to govern their deployment. Determined to prevail in Vietnam and increasingly alarmed by the reports of steady military and political decline, in July he approved the immediate deployment of 50,000 troops to South Vietnam. Recognizing that this would not be enough, however, he privately agreed to commit another 50,000 before the end of the year, and implicitly, at least, he committed himself to furnish whatever additional forces might be needed later. Johnson also authorized Westmoreland to "commit U.S. troops to combat independent of or in conjunction with GVN forces in any situation . . . when . . . their use is necessary to strengthen the relative position of GVN forces." These decisions rank among the most important in the history of American involvement in Vietnam. In July 1965, Johnson made an open-ended commitment to employ American military forces as the situation demanded. And by giving Westmoreland a free hand, he cleared the way for the United States to assume the burden of fighting in South Vietnam.[14]

This was the beginning of the war for the United States. In Vietnam it meant the beginning of the offensive "search and destroy" mission. "The July decisions—the closest thing to a formal decision for war in Vietnam—represented the culmination of a year and a half of agonizing on America's Vietnam policy and stemmed logically from the administration's refusal to accept the consequences of withdrawal."[15] Those consequences would violate the view of the world the United States had through the containment doctrine, the Truman Doctrine, the Domino Theory, and the SEATO treaty. The ability for the president to make the July decisions to go to combat status flowed from the Gulf of Tonkin Resolution. The year 1965 can be viewed as the year that changed the U.S. role in the war from that of adviser to combatant. It is also the first of many years of America's longest war.

Sam Donaldson said on *This Week with David Brinkley,* on April 30, 1995: "I think in that era no president could have stayed out of Vietnam at the outset."

U.S. ground strategy as the war escalated was to gradually wear down and diminish the enemy. This is called a strategy of attrition. What evolved out of the attrition strategy was the search and destroy mission. The objective of this type of mission was to find the North Vietnamese and Vietcong troops, engage them, and destroy them using superior U.S. firepower, be it from the ground or if necessary from the air. Search and destroy was not Gen. William Westmoreland's first phase. His first phase was to reverse the momentum of communist dominance by strengthening the defensive capabilities of the South and limited offensive actions by U.S. forces to reverse North Vietnam's forward thrust. It was hoped that this would be accomplished by the end of 1965.

Phase 2 would then employ search and destroy tactics in 1966. This phase would amount to massing a huge military force and logistical network to support it and beginning to confront the Vietcong and North Vietnamese. It was hoped this phase would be concluded by late 1966 or early 1967. If by that time the enemy had not been persuaded to a negotiated peace, phase 3 would be implemented. Phase 3 would be an all-out offensive to destroy the enemy. It was estimated that this phase would last a year and a half, thereby ending the war by the latter half of 1968.

It should also be noted that the military preferred an all-out air offensive against North Vietnam. Political considerations inhibited this as civilian leaders felt they were engaging in a balancing act already. That balancing act was to exert maximum military force against the enemy without causing Chinese and/or Soviet entrance into the conflict.

As 1965 came to a close there were 180,000 U.S. military personnel in Vietnam. General Westmoreland had made it clear that he wanted another 250,000 troops in the coming year, and President Johnson had made it clear that he could have them. U.S., South Vietnamese, Vietcong, and North Vietnamese casualties had increased. The air war over the North had increased, and North Vietnamese infiltration of troops and matériel down the Ho Chi Minh Trail (a series of roads and spurs from North Vietnam, through Laos and Cambodia, into South Vietnam) had increased. There was no sign, at this point, that there was any willingness on the part of the North or the Vietcong to negotiate.[16]

During 1966 and 1967 the U.S. military buildup and the war of attrition continued. By the end of 1966 there were approximately 280,000 U.S. troops in Vietnam, and the buildup continued to be matched by communist buildups. It was estimated that there were now 275,000 troops, including 45,000 North Vietnamese regulars, in South Vietnam. While U.S. forces inflicted heavy casualties on the enemy, this enemy continued to control the tempo and moment of the war. Communist forces largely picked and chose when to engage and when to melt into the population or jungle. They many times

66

thwarted the U.S. desire to bring superior firepower on them. "The North's principal tactic was to draw American units into close-quarter fighting to reduce the effectiveness of superior firepower."[17]

The year of 1967 was a year of continued military buildup on both sides. U.S. forces increased from about 380,000 at the beginning of the year to approximately 500,000 at the end of the year. It was estimated that the enemy had regular forces of about 250,000 and a similar number of irregular and political unit forces. South Vietnamese forces numbered approximately 200,000. Allied forces (U.S., South Vietnamese, and others) had an absolute numerical advantage. This numerical advantage, however, was nowhere near the accepted ratio of 10:1 or more generally accepted as needed to defeat a largely guerrilla army.

The war had become more costly also. Cost of the war for the United States at the end of the fiscal year ending June 1967 had been about $21 billion. The number of U.S. soldiers killed in action in 1967 was 9,353, which was more than all the previous years of the war combined. As the cost of the war mounted in terms of casualties and money, opposition to the war increased also. This occurred in Congress and "back on the block" as well.

By the end of 1967, however, U.S. officials were encouraged with the progress of the war. In the fall of 1967 South Vietnam had held elections. Despite the attempts of the Viet Cong to sabotage the elections, approximately 51 percent of the electorate turned out and elected Nguyen Van Thieu president of South Vietnam. The fact that these elections had been held encouraged the U.S. officials. It also was generally considered that the war in the field was being won. There was optimistic talk of the "light at the end of the tunnel" and other such phraseology. Gen. William Westmoreland led the charge of official optimism.

Westmoreland judged the military situation near the end of 1967 secure enough to take time out in November, at the request of the White House, to accompany Ambassador Ellsworth Bunker to the United States and confer with President Johnson and to "campaign" for the war effort. Westmoreland would not disappoint the administration. Even as he stepped from an air force jet in Washington he described the situation in Vietnam as "very, very encouraging . . . I have never been more encouraged in my four years in Vietnam." In addition, General Westmoreland would repeat his optimism before both the House and Senate Armed Services Committees, on television, and in his speeches.[18]

Westmoreland exuded optimism on NBC's *Meet the Press* and in a speech at the National Press Club in Washington, D.C., on November 21, 1967. He said that we had reached an important point where the end had come into view. He gave the impression that we had already entered phase 3 of his military plan, which was the victory phase, and he talked of a new phase, phase 4, which had not been included in his 1965 plan. This phase 4, considered to be a mopping up of Vietnamese communists, was projected to progress sufficiently within two years to begin withdrawing U.S. troops.[19] Westmoreland stated, "We are making progress. We know you want an honorable and early transition to the fourth and last phase. So do your sons and so do I. It lies within our grasp—the enemy's hopes are bankrupt. With your support we will give you a success that will impact not only on South Vietnam, but on every emerging nation in the world."[20]

As 1968 unfolded, the optimism of the end of 1967 faded and the situation developed in a different fashion than had been envisioned by many Washington policy makers. Nineteen-sixty-eight was a pivotal year in the Vietnam War, and an event called the Tet Offensive launched by the Vietcong and

North Vietnamese army drastically altered the course of the war.

Tet is a traditional Vietnamese holiday, the holiday that signals the beginning of the lunar New Year. Traditionally during the war it was customary to observe a cease-fire during these holidays. In 1968 the NLF (Vietcong) had called for a cease-fire and asked for scrupulous observance of the holiday. The government of South Vietnam and the United States agreed to the cease-fire.

There had been intelligence reports that the communists might take advantage of the holiday to launch an attack, but the general feeling was that there would not be a general offensive. On January 31, 1968, a general offensive *was* launched by the communists in violation of the cease-fire, and the offensive created much havoc initially in South Vietnam. The Vietcong and North Vietnamese seized partial control or used terrorist tactics against twenty-six of South Vietnam's provincial capitals. Communists even assaulted the U.S. embassy in Saigon and penetrated to within the walls before they were destroyed. The offensive received widespread media coverage in the United States, and the initial media reports gave the impression that U.S. and South Vietnamese forces had been surprised and defeated. Surprised, yes; defeated, no! After the initial successes the Vietcong and the North Vietnamese scored, the tide was turned and a victory for the Americans and their allies occurred. The Vietcong infrastructure was destroyed, and its forces were increasingly replaced by North Vietnamese Regulars. Walter Cronkite has stated, "It is believed that the enemy lost at least fifty-eight thousand dead during Tet and perhaps three times that many wounded. The communist death toll was roughly six times that of American, South Vietnamese, and other friendly forces."[21]

The Vietcong and the North Vietnamese had expected the South Vietnamese people to engage in a "general uprising." It was believed that the people would join with them to defeat the South Vietnamese government and the U.S. forces supporting it. The general uprising did not occur, and the South Vietnamese army performed in a better-than-expected fashion during the Tet Offensive.

At face value it seemed that the United States had achieved success during Tet. "But if the United States had won tactically, it suffered a fatal strategic blow. False expectations had been raised at home that the war had been virtually won."[22] The ability of the enemy to engage in an offensive as massive as Tet had made U.S. people feel betrayed and lied to concerning the progress of the war.

> The Tet Offensive cost the government and the military the confidence of the American people. Not only did the American public turn further against the war, but the Commander-in-Chief, President Johnson, seemed psychologically defeated by the Tet Offensive. Challenged within his own party for renomination and with public support slipping away, he thereafter publicly announced that he would not seek reelection.[23]

The war would continue for another seven years, but it would never be the same. Tet changed the war and the American perception of it.

The immediate impact of Tet was that on President Johnson and his decision to not seek reelection. By the end of March 1968 Johnson announced that the United States would limit its bombing to invasion routes and areas just to the north of the Demilitarized Zone (DMZ) separating North and South Vietnam. In a nationally televised speech on March 31, 1968, Johnson announced that the remainder of his term would be devoted to the duties of the presidency, one of which would be to seek a settlement of the Vietnam War:

With America's sons in the fields far away, with America's future under challenge right here at home, with our hopes and the world's hopes for peace in the balance every day, I do not believe that I should devote an hour or a day of my time to any other than the awesome duties of this office—the presidency of your country.

Accordingly, I shall not seek, and I will not accept, the nomination of my party for another term as your president.[24]

The North Vietnamese government in Hanoi responded to Johnson's bombing reductions with a positive response to beginning negotiations for peace. In May 1968 the United States and North Vietnam began these talks in Paris. After much haggling, the NLF and the government of the Republic of South Vietnam were included in the peace talks.

While peace talks were occurring, the war continued in 1968 and later. The Democrats nominated Hubert Humphrey for president, and the Republicans nominated Richard M. Nixon. The election was won by Nixon, and there was a general sense that he had both a plan and a mandate to bring the war quickly to an end.[25]

The Nixon plan for the war in Vietnam was called Vietnamization. This consisted of a gradual turning over of the war to South Vietnamese. As the Southern forces were built up with our supplies and were able to take on a greater responsibility for the war, U.S. forces would be withdrawn from Vietnam. The first reductions were announced on June 8, 1969, as President Nixon ordered the withdrawal of 25,000 troops. By the end of 1969 Nixon had reduced U.S. troop strength in Vietnam from a peak of 543,000 in June to 479,000. The South Vietnamese were enlarging their army from 850,000 to 1 million during this time period. The South Vietnamese were taking on a greater share of the fighting, and U.S. forces had reduced offensive operations. Vast quantities of U.S. equipment were also being turned over to the South Vietnamese armed forces.

It was during 1969 that President Nixon also enunciated the Nixon Doctrine, which basically said that the United States would honor its commitments when its allies were threatened with external attack, but the primary responsibility for the defense of the threatened nation would be with its own manpower. The Nixon Doctrine obviously philosophically complemented the policy of Vietnamization.

The Paris Peace Talks had continued in 1969 and also continued in 1970 without much progress. Henry Kissinger, who was national security adviser at this time, began secret talks in Paris with the communists. Vietnamization continued throughout the year. In order to hasten Vietnamization, President Nixon ordered U.S. troops into Cambodia in late April to destroy North Vietnamese and Vietcong sanctuaries in that country. Nixon stated that the United States was not widening the war and that the Cambodian incursion would only last until communist staging areas used to launch operations into South Vietnam had been destroyed. All U.S. forces were to be out of Cambodia by the end of June. Nixon put it this way: "Finally, on April 30 I announced our decision to counter the communist offensive by attacking North Vietnamese–occupied base areas in Cambodia bordering on South Vietnam. Our principal purpose was to undercut the North Vietnamese invasion of that country so that Vietnamization and plans for the withdrawal of American troops could continue in South Vietnam."[26]

Nixon kept his promise to limit the invasion of Cambodia. U.S. ground operations were ended by the end of June. Unfortunately, the incursion into Cambodia had been viewed on college campuses as a widening of the war. It reignited antiwar demonstrators in a wave of demonstrations. The worst incident, of course, was the killing of four students at Kent State University.

By the end of 1970 the war had continued winding down for Americans. Troop strength had been reduced to 270,000, and the war had reverted to a seemingly earlier phase, with U.S. casualties being reduced and those that were occurring being caused by such actions as enemy booby traps and sniper fire.

While the air war had been largely discontinued over most of North Vietnam, it continued in areas of South Vietnam and in communist-controlled areas of Laos and Cambodia during 1971. When the decision to stop bombing in North Vietnam was made in 1968 there also were some tacit understandings about the conduct of the war. One of these was that U.S. reconnaissance flights would continue over the North. "When these aircraft were fired upon, the Seventh Air Force was authorized to strike North Vietnamese air defense installations. This authorization allowed attacks on North Vietnamese air defenses, known as 'protective reaction strikes,' as soon as their radar guidance systems locked in on American aircraft."[27] Protective reaction strikes occurred in January, February, and March in and just to the north of the DMZ as well as in Laotian border areas.

In December 1971 the sharpest escalation of the air war since saturation bombing ended in 1968 occurred. U.S. fighter bombers struck at North Vietnamese airfields, missile sites, antiaircraft emplacements, and supply facilities for five straight days. On December 27, U.S. defense secretary Melvin Laird said that the stepup was in retaliation for the communist failure to live up to the tacit agreements prior to the 1968 bombing halt. He cited the shelling of Saigon the week before, the building of an infiltration route through the DMZ buffer zone, and attacks on unarmed U.S. reconnaissance planes.[28] This series of strikes also fell under the protective reaction category.

Continued Vietnamization occurred in the ground war in 1971. U.S. mechanized forces were removed from their position just two miles south of the DMZ, and this position was taken over by the South Vietnamese army. U.S. troop levels that were at 270,000 at the start of the year had been reduced to 159,000 at the end of the year. Virtually all combat responsibility had been turned over to the South Vietnamese.

Nineteen seventy-two was a year of stalled on and off secret and nonsecret negotiations in Paris. Both sides were jockeying for position as it became apparent that U.S. involvement was coming to an end. The communists wanted to have a decisive military blow that would impact on the American elections and show that Vietnamization would not work. To accomplish this they launched their Easter offensive on March 30. About 120,000 North Vietnamese Regulars and thousands of Vietcong struck in the northern provinces, the central highlands, and the Cambodian border areas near Saigon. The fighting was furious between enemy and forces of South Vietnam, and the offensive lasted into June 1972.

To aid the South Vietnamese, the United States continued air support in the South and launched Operation Linebacker I. This operation consisted of U.S. Air Force, Marine, and Navy aircraft flying some forty-one thousand sorties over North Vietnam. They used B-52 strategic bombers as well as navy mine-laying aircraft. North Vietnamese harbors were mined and closed to oceangoing traffic; ten MIG air bases were destroyed, as well as six major power plants and all large oil storage facilities in North Vietnam.[29] The communists were denied their decisive military victory with the offensive. "U.S. mining of Haiphong Harbor and the use of our airpower against targets in North Vietnam helped save the day, but the fighting on the ground was done exclusively by South Vietnamese forces. North Vietnam lost an estimated 130,000 killed and disabled. The invasion was a failure."[30]

Linebacker I ended in the fall of 1972, and negotiations in Paris continued on and off. By December of 1972 the Paris Peace Talks again stalemated. In the face of this perceived intransigence by the communists, Pres. Richard Nixon ordered Operation Linebacker II.

On December 18, 1972, Linebacker Two began, and for a period of eleven days U.S. aircraft unleashed the heaviest bombing raids of the entire war, dropping almost 40,000 tons of bombs on the heavily populated region between Hanoi and Haiphong. The Christmas bombings, as these raids became known, were remarkable for the low level of casualties, but they did succeed in forcing the communists to return to the negotiating table.[31]

The year 1972 came to a close. It had been one of the most destructive years of the war. U.S. combat forces were reduced to 24,000 by the end of the year. This number is a small fraction of the peak troop commitment of approximately 550,000 that the United States had in 1968–69. Surely America's Vietnam War was near to an end.

In early January 1973 peace negotiations were resumed in Paris. By January 15 President Nixon, due to progress in the peace negotiations, suspended the bombing, mining, shelling, and all other offensive action against North Vietnam. On January 23 President Nixon announced that Henry Kissinger, U.S. secretary of state, and Le Duc Tho, North Vietnamese negotiator, had initialed an agreement that a cease-fire was to go into effect on January 28, Saigon time. The cease-fire was stated "to end the war and bring peace with honor in Vietnam and Southeast Asia."[32]

The main points of the Paris agreement for a cease-fire were the following:

- A cease-fire throughout Vietnam.
- Withdrawal of all U.S. troops and advisers within sixty days.
- The dismantling of all U.S. bases within sixty days.
- Release of all U.S. and other prisoners of war within sixty days.
- Continuance in place of North Vietnamese troops in South Vietnam.
- Withdrawal of all foreign troops from Laos and Cambodia and prohibition of bases in and troop movement through these countries.
- Agreement that the DMZ at the seventeenth parallel would remain a provisional dividing line with eventual reunification of the country "through peaceful means."
- Establishment of an international commission to supervise the agreement.
- Continuance of South Vietnamese Nguyen Van Thieu in office pending elections.
- Respect by North Vietnam for the South Vietnamese people's right to self-determination.
- No military movement across the DMZ.
- No use of force to reunify the country.[33]

On March 29, 1973, the last U.S. troops left South Vietnam. A Defense Attaché Office, a few marine embassy guards in Saigon, and about eighty-five hundred U.S. civilians remained in the South. America's war in Vietnam seemed to be over.

While the war was over for the United States, the war was not over. All the Paris peace agreements established was a framework for continuing the war without direct U.S. involvement. North Vietnam still desired to unify the country on its own terms. South Vietnam struggled on to survive as an independent nation with the support of some U.S. officials, including President Nixon, sharing the South's aspirations. The cease-fire existed on paper only. The last phase of the war lasted for a very short duration. South Vietnam had difficulty functioning on its own, as President Nixon was not allowed by Congress to live up to the promises that he had made to Thieu. Eventually, of course, Nixon was forced to resign from the presidency as a result of Watergate. Congress drastically cut back aid to South Vietnam, further eroding its will to resist. When the North Vietnamese launched a major offensive in 1975, South Vietnam fell very rapidly.[34]

If the Paris agreement were to succeed it would had to have been enforced to deter Hanoi from breaking it. President Nixon had stated in a private letter to President Thieu that "if Hanoi fails to abide by the terms of this agreement, it is my intention to take swift and severe retaliatory action."[35]

Violations had occurred, but Nixon, weakened by Watergate, was able to only *threaten* retaliatory action. In August 1973 Congress passed a bill setting August 15 as the date for the cessation of bombing of sanctuary areas in Cambodia and mandating congressional approval of funding for any military action in Indochina. "The effect of this bill was to deny the President the means to enforce the Vietnam peace agreement by retaliating against Hanoi for violations."[36]

Executive powers of Nixon and later President Ford to enforce the Paris agreement were further weakened in November 1973 with the War Powers Resolution. That resolution requires consultation with Congress and time limitations on troop deployment by the executive. All of this activity had been monitored in Hanoi, of course.

During 1974 the Soviets were pouring massive amounts of military aid into North Vietnam, which in turn supplied its forces in the South with these materials. "At the same time that the Soviet Union was arming Hanoi for the final assault, the United States Congress was sharply curtailing the flow of aid to

South Vietnam. U.S. aid was halved in 1974 and cut by another third in 1975."[37]

Original North Vietnamese timing for their all-out offensive to conquer South Vietnam was for 1976. Events, as they unfolded, caused the North to advance their timetable. On August 9, 1974, Richard Nixon resigned from the presidency of the United States. Gerald Ford succeeded Nixon and did not really have the experience to deal with the Vietnam problem. Congress was also not in a mood of cooperation with the executive, having just forced the removal of a president from office for the first time in U.S. history. In late December 1974 and early January 1975 the North took Phuoc Long Province, which is just northeast of Saigon. They were emboldened by the lack of response by the United States and decided to accelerate their attacks. On March 11 Ban Me Thout, a South Vietnamese stronghold in the Central Highlands, fell. The same day, the U.S. Congress refused to fund a supplemental military aid package that President Ford had requested.[38]

These cutbacks in aid devastated South Vietnam's morale as well as denying them the supplies they were desperately short of to defend themselves. The North sensed the situation and threw its troops into an all-out offensive. The rout was on and occurred with a rapidity that surprised all parties involved. The army of the Republic of South Vietnam made a stand at Xuan Loc, the last line of defense before Saigon, and was defeated. Saigon fell to the North Vietnamese on April 30, 1975, as Duong Van Minh, representing the South, surrendered unconditionally to the communist forces. All the remaining non-combat Americans exited before the communist forces entered the city. Many South Vietnamese fled at this time also, but many who wished to flee were unable to do so.

Thus it was that two years after U.S. combat forces left South Vietnam it fell to the communists. The struggle that had emerged after World War II and included increasing and then decreasing U.S. combat troops over a period of eight years finally ended in 1975 without the presence of the U.S. military. The U.S. attempt at nation building in South Vietnam had not succeeded.

The Vietnam War was more divisive in the United States than any war since the Civil War. The logic of U.S. involvement in the war has been explained and, I hope, understood. Whether the logic was sound will be debated into the future. ABC News commentator George Will put it this way on *This Week with David Brinkley* on April 30, 1995: "I think the final judgement on Vietnam has yet to be written." ***This writer agrees!***

Notes

1. Guenter Lewy, *America in Vietnam* (New York: Oxford University Press, 1978), p. 36.
2. Robert McNamara, *In Retrospect, the Tragedy and Lessons of Vietnam* (New York: Random House, 1995), p. 151.
3. Tony Murdoch, Joan M. Crouse, and Pam O'Connell, *Vietnam* (White Plains, NY: Longman, 1994), p. 94.
4. Ibid.
5. McNamara, *In Retrospect,* pp. 167–68.
6. Murdoch, Crouse, and O'Connell, *Vietnam,* p. 95.
7. Ibid.
8. Lewy, *America in Vietnam,* p. 40.
9. Ibid.
10. "Aggression from the North": *State Department White Paper on Vietnam,* February 27, 1965 (Department of State Bulletin, March 22, 1965).
11. McNamara, *In Retrospect,* p. 174.
12. Ibid., p. 179.
13. Murdoch, Crouse, and O'Connell, *Vietnam,* p. 96.
14. George C. Herring, *America's Longest War: The United States and Vietnam* (New York: McGraw-Hill, 1986), p. 139.
15. Herring, *America's Longest War,* p. 141.
16. John S. Bowman, *The Vietnam War: An Almanac* (New York: World Almanac, 1985), p. 158.

17. Murdoch, Crouse, and O'Connell, *Vietnam,* p. 110.
18. Edward Doyle and Samuel Lipsman, eds., *The Vietnam Experience, America Takes Over, 1965–1967* (Boston: Boston Publishing Company, 1982), p. 182.
19. Neil Sheehan, *A Bright Shining Lie, John Paul Vann and America in Vietnam* (New York: Random House, 1988), pp. 698–99.
20. William Westmoreland speech as quoted in ibid., p. 699.
21. Videotape, *The Vietnam War with Walter Cronkite, the Tet Offensive* (New York: CBS News, 1985).
22. Harry G. Summers, Jr., *Vietnam War Almanac* (New York: Facts on File, 1985), p. 335.
23. Ibid., p. 335.
24. United States Government, *Public Papers of the Presidents of the United States: Lyndon B. Johnson, 1968* (Washington, 1970), pp. 469–76.
25. Bowman, *The Vietnam War,* p. 218.
26. Richard Nixon, *The Real War* (New York: Warner, 1980), p.108.
27. Summers, *Vietnam War Almanac,* p.227.
28. Bowman, *The Vietnam War,* p. 294.
29. Summers, *Vietnam War Almanac,* p. 228.
30. Nixon, *The Real War,* p. 112.
31. Murdoch, Crouse, and O'Connell, *Vietnam,* p. 157.
32. Bowman, *The Vietnam War,* p. 337.
33. Ibid., p. 338.
34. Herring, *America's Longest War,* p. 257.
35. Nixon, *The Real War,* p. 116.
36. Ibid., p. 117.
37. Ibid.
38. Ibid., p. 118.

Part II

Introduction

As stated in the preface, part 2 of this book will tend to be more controversial and subjective than part 1. It should be reiterated that the reader probably will have been exposed and subjected to information concerning certain topics related to the Vietnam War so many times and by so many sources that the information has led to "conclusions" and "lessons" that have become "givens." These givens have been repeated over and over to the point that they have taken on a self-sustaining credibility.

Part 2 of this book will explore many of the topics concerning these givens and expose the reader to information about them that is not necessarily consistent with what the reader has read, heard, or seen. This exposure will, I hope, allow the reader to make better-informed and more thoughtful judgments about the conclusions and lessons that have been accepted and perpetuated concerning these topics related to a very controversial war. The reader may very well return to original beliefs concerning subjects, and that is just as well, too. At least the reader will know that there **are** some different perspectives concerning these matters.

Historically, the presentation of U.S. history in textbooks, in U.S. classrooms, in the media, and in public discussion has had a marked tendency to accentuate the positive and to even slant history to portray American military efforts in a better light than they realistically were. This was done to a degree in the name of patriotism. There were and always have been the critics and detractors concerning America's military involvements, but for the most part they were a small minority and not in the mainstream.

It is this book's contention that, for whatever reason, the experience of the Vietnam War internationally and the Watergate scandal domestically changed the tendency to bias things in a positive light. At some point in the Vietnam War, it became the norm to exercise bias in the opposite direction. The war became unpopular, and the conclusions in the media, classrooms, textbooks, and entertainment fields began to reflect this perspective. These conclusions are now, for the most part, viewed as factual history and are being passed down through the generations as historical fact. There has been a conscious and an unconscious effort by those who turned against the Vietnam War to perpetuate their conclusions for posterity. This effort has accorded those who have shaped the history of the Vietnam war a postwar vindication of the antiwar attitudes they embraced during the war.

Given this, part 2 of this book will attempt to show some erroneous givens that are being perpetuated and offer evidence for alternative conclusions. It also will demonstrate, with some examples, conscious or unconscious errors in portraying topics and incidents of the Vietnam War. Many of these examples will be as current as within the last few years (early to mid-nineties).

A rapid way to find out how history is being portrayed is to see what is being written in textbooks. This is particularly true of high school textbooks, as high school is where this country attempts to inform the majority of its population of America's history. Part 2 will relate to the reader what some mainstream high school textbooks are saying about the Vietnam War and contrast this with other sources.

Similarly, other sources of information and mainstream conclusions will be examined as to how they have portrayed and continue to portray topics concerning the Vietnam War.

These portrayals will be contrasted with other conclusions and positions in an effort to strike a balance from differing points of view.

One of the topics will be an examination of Ho Chi Minh and the question of his communism versus his nationalism. An examination of the nature of the war, as to whether it was a civil war or an invasion from the North, will occur as well as aspects of U.S. military involvement. The questions surrounding the Tet Offensive, the Cambodian invasion, the alleged "unique horror" of the Vietnam war, and the portrayal of the U.S. soldier will be explored. The book will conclude with an examination of the role the antiwar movement played in the war.

5

Ho Chi Minh: Nationalist or Communist?

A thorough discussion of the issues surrounding the Vietnam War must address the nature of Ho Chi Minh. Was Ho an ardent international communist revolutionary, or was he simply a Vietnamese nationalist, a "George Washington" of his country? This question needs to be discussed because it had ramifications for the foreign policy of the United States. If Ho was the international communist doing the bidding of the Soviet Union, the repercussions for U.S. foreign policy should have been fashioned to address that situation. If Ho was simply a Vietnamese nationalist, U.S. foreign policy should have responded differently than it would have in the former case.

This book will define nationalism, as opposed to internationalism, as giving priority to national rather than international goals. U.S. foreign policy experts deemed Ho to be the international communist in the 1950s and early sixties, while in later times it has seemed to become fashionable in most circles to view Ho as the Vietnamese nationalist.

One thing that appears to be true about Ho Chi Minh is that relatively little seems to be known about the man. Knowledge of Ho is minute when contrasted to knowledge of other wartime adversaries of the United States such as Hitler and Mussolini in World War II or even the German Kaiser in World War I. This is apparent despite the fact that the Vietnam War was the longest in our history and probably has more footage of film and written word than the rest of our wars. It would be interesting to observe U.S. knowledge of Saddam Hussein if Desert Storm had continued for a longer period of time. It is probable that there would be a much greater wealth of information on Saddam. Ho Chi Minh and Kim Il Sung (Korean War) have been relegated to the relative vacuum bin of U.S. historical knowledge.

U.S. high school textbooks devote a relatively small portion of their content to the background of Ho. This is unfortunate, because more background information would help determine the nationalist-versus-international-communist question. Some of the content the textbooks do devote to Ho's background can also be challenged as to its validity.

The extent of coverage of Ho by the textbook *The National Experience* is limited to one sentence: "Ho was a nationalist as well as a Communist, and the Viet Minh were seen by most Indochinese as a movement for national independence."[1] In this text, Ho is referred to as a nationalist first, then a communist.

In the textbook *American Voices, a History of the United States, 1865 to the Present* coverage of background is very limited: "The nationalist leader was Ho Chi Minh, a communist educated in Paris and Moscow, who was determined to win independence for his nation."[2] While brief in background coverage, this text appears to accentuate the nationalist aspect more than the communist.

The textbook *These United States, the Questions of Our Past* contains greater, but not in-depth, coverage of the issue. It says: "Ho Chi Minh, a Communist nationalist, refused to accept French rule."[3] This textbook then continues on in an attempt to downplay Ho's expansionist tendencies, which would seemingly support his nationalist tendencies. What the textbook says, paradoxically, challenges the validity of Ho's **Vietnamese** nationalist credentials.

Dealing with Ho is put into the context of Western dealings with Hitler at Munich. At Munich, of course, Western leaders followed a policy of appeasement. They gave in to Hitler's demands and thereby encouraged him to be even more aggressive and expansionist. "Applied to Vietnam, this analogy meant that if Communist forces were allowed to conquer South Vietnam, one by one the other non-aligned or pro-Western nations of Southeast Asia would fall to Communist control."[4]

In an attempt to refute this previous logic and context, this textbook unwittingly harms Ho's nationalist credentials: "This logic was faulty. Ho Chi Minh was not ruler of a powerful militarized nation such as Germany. Ho's ally, the Soviet Union, might have expansionist tendencies of uncertain dimensions, but there was no evidence that Ho himself had designs on any part of Asia beyond former Indochina."[5]

Indochina consisted of the countries of Vietnam, Cambodia, and Laos. The previous quote alludes to the fact that Ho had designs on Laos and Cambodia as parts of Indochina, thereby challenging his Vietnamese nationalist credentials.

This point of view that Ho had designs on all of Indochina is supported by other sources. "Ho, in fact, always considered his leadership to extend to Indochina as a whole, and his party was originally called the Indochinese Communist Party."[6]

The textbook *Todd & Curti's The American Nation* gives much more extensive coverage of Ho Chi Minh's background than the other textbooks mentioned. It also bolsters his nationalist credentials: "Foremost among nationalists was Nguyen That Thanh, a world wanderer and a man of many names, whose last alias was Ho Chi Minh—'He who enlightens.' "[7] *Todd & Curti's* goes on to say: "From London, Ho went to Paris, where he soon emerged as a leader of Vietnamese nationalists living in France."[8]

There are those who would challenge that Ho was the "foremost among nationalists" of that time period. During the first third of this century a man named Phan Boi Chau was the foremost Vietnamese nationalist. "Phan, who has been characterized by the late Bernard Fall as 'Vietnam's Sun Yat-sen,' is today considered a national hero in both North and South Vietnam."[9] "Directly, or indirectly through his teachings, during the first quarter of this century he was responsible for nearly every act of anti-French resistance in Vietnam."[10] Fall, of course, was writing while the war in Vietnam was still being fought, hence the reference to North and South Vietnam.

It is also difficult to accept Ho as Vietnam's foremost nationalist considering he spent the majority of his time between 1911 and 1941 wandering the world. Ho spent time in Great Britain, the United States, France, China, and the Soviet Union, to mention a few places.

Ho was born in central Vietnam in 1890. In 1911 he got a job as a cook on a French merchant ship. Later he settled in London and learned the English language. From London he went to Paris, where he helped organize the French Communist Party.

According to *Todd & Curti's The American Nation:*

> Later, Ho claimed that "it was patriotism and not Communism that originally inspired" his quest for independence. By 1923, though, he was convinced that a worldwide Communist revolution was Vietnam's only hope and left Paris to study revolutionary tactics in Moscow.
>
> During the 1920s and 1930s Ho organized and plotted for Vietnamese independence. One French comrade described him as "taut and quivering, with only one thought in his head, his country, Vietnam." Hunted as a Communist, Ho donned disguises as he moved from country to country—sometimes a Chinese journalist, at other times a Buddhist monk with flowing robes.
>
> What Ho awaited was a chance to launch his plan. That chance came during World War II. In 1940 the Japanese army

swept down from China to occupy all of French Indochina, the Philippines, Malaya, and Indonesia. In Vietnam the Japanese left the French colonial government in place but controlled it. Early in 1941 Ho slipped secretly into Vietnam to organize a resistance. He called the movement the League for the Independence of Vietnam, or Vietminh.[11]

The reader must be careful to not conclude from the previous quote that Ho spent the whole time period 1941–45 in Vietnam as an active resistance fighter against Japan. "Taking a new alias, Ho Chi Minh, he traveled to China in 1942 to seek help from the Chinese Nationalist government for operations against the Japanese. Arrested as a communist agent, he remained in jail until 1943, when he was released by the Chinese to organize an anti-Japanese resistance movement in Vietnam."[12]

It is very difficult to answer the question of nationalist versus communist by relying on these high school textbooks. It does appear that the textbooks alternatively mention both of them. The overall thrust also appears to omit anything negative concerning Ho and probably leans slightly to the nationalist definition.

There are other sources that attack Ho's nationalist credentials, however, and this book will relate some of those sources to the reader. This will be done by discussing events and occurrences in Ho's life in a chronological fashion and exposing some not-too-well-known information.

Ho's time in France in the twenties was followed by time in the Soviet Union and then China. "After later study in the Soviet Union he was assigned as a Comintern agent in China in 1925."[13] It was during this time that one of the events that challenges Ho's nationalist credentials occurred.

"The Comintern, or Communist International, was a world organization of Communist parties under the leadership of the Communist Party of the USSR. . . . It dictated policies to the Communist parties in the other countries, deploying them in the service of the Soviet state."[14] It should be emphasized that Ho was an agent of the Comintern, an organization that did the bidding of the Soviet Union. This hardly strengthens the nationalist argument for him.

Phan Boi Chau, Vietnam's foremost nationalist, was in China at this time also. "The French authorities in Vietnam were disturbed by Phan Boi Chau's activities, and for twenty years he was forced to flee from country to country to elude French agents."[15]

> Phan was the number one target of the French colonial authorities because of his revolutionary activities, and they were happy to pay Ho Chi Minh 100,000 piasters for Phan's betrayal. Ho sent Phan an invitation to meet and discuss ways for the two to work together in furthering the anti-French resistance movement, and to participate in the founding of the Vietnamese branch of the World Federation of Small and Weak Nations. When the invitation was accepted, Ho informed the French who intercepted Phan at the Shanghai railway station and returned him to Haiphong for trial.[16]

Ho of course felt it necessary to justify Phan's betrayal to his communist associates. According to P. J. Honey, Ho gave these three reasons as justification:

1. Phan Boi Chau was a Nationalist, not a Communist, and would prove to be a rival to the Communists in their plan to take control of the Vietnamese anti-French resistance movement. In betraying him he had disposed of a future rival.
2. The reward money which he had received from the French could be put to excellent use in forwarding the Vietnamese Communist movement.

3. The execution of Phan Boi Chau would create the required atmosphere of shock and resentment inside Vietnam.[17]

"Phan Boi Chau was tried and on 23 November 1925 sentenced to death. Because of widespread public protest, the sentence was commuted to life imprisonment and finally to life under house arrest."[18] Ho Chi Minh eliminated a future rival in this devious fashion, even if that rival was Vietnam's foremost nationalist. Ho did this to promote the future of the communist movement!

In mid-1925 Ho Chi Minh founded the Vietnam Association of Young Revolutionaries. A handful of the very hard-core of this group were gathered into a communist group, Tan Viet.[19] The Tan Viet was also known as Thanh Nien. Almost simultaneously the VNQDD was being established. "The Vietnam Quoc Dan Dong (VNQDD) was mainly an urban, middle class group that favored a republican government and an end to French control."[20]

"In addition to strengthening his own organization, Ho Chi Minh worked actively in the late 1920s to undermine Nationalist opposition. The VNQDD was founded in 1927, and within two years it grew to become numerically the strongest party in Vietnam."[21] The VNQDD was one of the organizations in Vietnam that sent future leaders of their parties to the Whampoa Academy in China for training. It is instructive to relate the activities of Ho in reference to what went on with these nationalists in China:

Upon arrival in Hong Kong or Canton, however, each new recruit for the academy was required to submit two photographs in order to complete his files. The Young Nationalists were approached at the academy by Ho or his agents and invited to abandon their parties and join the Thanh Nien. Those who accepted were allowed to return to Vietnam and became the nucleus around which Ho would later build a Leninist party. The Nationalists rejecting the invitation never returned to their organizations inside Vietnam. Ho arranged for their photographs and travel plans to fall into French hands, and they were arrested upon crossing the border. The money Ho obtained from the French for these betrayals was used to further his Communist activities in Canton. Thus he financed his operations and eliminated his future competition at the same time.[22]

Once again, the apparent priority of Ho Chi Minh seemed very clear. Ho was willing to betray fellow nationalists in the most devious ways to move communists to the forefront of the struggle against the French.

In 1930 two significant events occurred. One of them was the massive damage of the VNQDD when the French crushed a rebellion by the nationalists at Yen Bay. This defeat was significant because it saw the leadership of the Vietnamese nationalist movement now pass into the hands of procommunist groups. The second event was the founding of the Vietnamese Communist Party in 1930. More specifically, the Indochinese Communist Party (ICP) was founded in 1929. This was followed by the formation of the Annamese Communist Party in the South and the Tan Viet Communist League in central Vietnam. Ho merged the three into the Vietnamese Communist Party in 1930.

Ho spent the thirties outside Vietnam. He organized the Far Eastern Bureau of the Comintern and was arrested and imprisoned by the British authorities in Hong Kong. Ho was able to escape the British and went into southern China. He also spent time studying in the Soviet Union again. "Returning to Moscow in 1938, he was one of the few Comintern agents to survive the Stalinist purges underway there."[23] It can only be speculated as to what strength of ideologically pure status Ho embodied to survive the inquisitions of Stalin.

As mentioned earlier, with Japanese occupation of Vietnam Ho was able to slip back into the country and establish the League for the Independence of Vietnam, or Vietminh, as they were known.

Following Stalin's example (who earlier had downplayed communism in favor of Mother Russia to win public support for the "great patriotic war" against the Nazis), Ho Chi Minh proclaimed his anti-Japanese and anti-French Vietminh as a nationalist rather than a communist movement and ostensibly dissolved the Indochina Communist Party in November 1945. Like Russia's "Uncle Joe," he became Vietnam's "Uncle Ho."[24]

It also was discussed earlier how Ho went to China to gain support, was imprisoned there until 1943, and then returned to Vietnam. During the time period of 1943–45 he worked in resistance to the Japanese. His work brought him into contact with the U.S. OSS, and he used these contacts to politically benefit himself later.

After the Japanese were defeated, Ho proclaimed himself president of the newly independent Vietnam in the so-called August Revolution of 1945. "Earlier Ho had used his contacts with American OSS agents to convince his political opponents (including Emperor Bao Dai, who abdicated in Ho's favor) that he alone enjoyed the support of the United States, thereby enabling him to seize control of the Vietnamese nationalist movement."[25]

By 1946 the French were ready to return to Indochina to restore colonial control. Ho Chi Minh by 1946 had maneuvered himself into almost total political power in Vietnam. At this point Ho did not confront the French but worked out a compromise with them. Events surrounding this situation will be examined in an evaluation of Ho's nationalist credentials.

Back in 1945, prior to Ho's August Revolution and declaration of independence for Vietnam, other forces in the world had been making decisions that would impact on the future of Vietnam. U.S. president Harry Truman and other Allied leaders had met at Potsdam a few weeks before Ho had declared independence and had reached certain decisions.

The Potsdam leaders had determined that Vietnam would be divided temporarily at the sixteenth parallel at the end of the war. North of that boundary, Chinese nationalists were to handle the surrender of Japanese forces, to arrange for their repatriation to Japan, and to obtain the release of all prisoners of war. South of that line, the British would take care of similar matters. Secret agreements at Potsdam in effect also granted the French a free hand to return to Indochina and reimpose their colonialism in Vietnam. By 1946 Ho Chi Minh had his government in northern Vietnam, the Chinese were still occupying the area, and the French had designs on moving back in.[26]

An agreement was reached on 28 February 1946 between the Nationalist Chinese occupying Vietnam north of the 16th parallel and the French, providing for the replacement by 15 March of all Chinese troops in Vietnam by French soldiers. This placed the Vietminh in a dilemma: They had yet to consolidate fully their position of supremacy within the revolutionary movement, and they were not by themselves strong enough to effectively resist the return of the French.

To be faithful to Lenin's admonition to fight only one enemy at a time, they were forced either (1) to reach an accommodation which would almost certainly require major concessions and run the risk of having to share power with the non-Communists; or (2) to reach a similar compromise with the French in order to buy time to neutralize the non-Communist elements which might challenge the Vietminh for leadership of the anti-French resistance. The choice was clearly one of priorities. Which was more important to the Communist leadership of the Viet Minh in 1946: success of the "National" or anti-French resistance, or firm Communist control of the resistance movement at the risk of prolonging or even losing the struggle? Predictably, Ho Chi Minh elected to pursue the second option.[27]

The compromise between the Viet Minh and the French consisted basically of two parts. First, the French recognized the Republic of Vietnam as a free state that could have its own government (including parliament, army, and treasury) and belonged to the Indochinese Federation and the French Union. Suffice it to say that the French and the Vietnamese later did not agree on how much autonomy this free state had within the French Union. Second, the Viet Minh declared itself ready to accept the presence of the French army.

Ho obviously was willing to reach a compromise with the French to solidify the communists at the expense of the nationalists. "Almost all members of the Nationalist opposition, both within the Ho Chi Minh government and outside of it, cried 'Betrayal!' but it was too late."[28]

Ho had historically attempted to eliminate other nationalists from positions to challenge his authority, and this had continued right after the August 1945 revolution. "During the period right after World War II the survivors of the Vietnam Kuomingtang and several other non-Communist factions attempted to set up rival administrations and militias in the North to contest the Viet Minh. Ho crushed them. About a hundred of the leaders were rounded up and executed."[29]

After the French and Vietminh reached their compromise in 1946 they worked together to eliminate Vietnamese nationalists. "This signalled the start of a major campaign conducted jointly and in close cooperation by Vietminh police and the

French, its aim to destroy the Nationalist organizations which had refused to welcome the return of the French to Vietnam."[30] "Hundreds of Nationalist leaders who might at some point in the future have provided guidance for a rival anti-French resistance movement were executed by the Vietminh during the campaign."[31]

Inevitably, the compromise agreement between the French and the Viet Minh did not endure. War between the Vietnamese and the French was carried on from 1946 until 1954, and as described elsewhere in this book, the Vietminh soundly defeated the French at Dien Bien Phu. This defeat caused the French to be driven out of Vietnam and a convening of the Geneva conference that resulted in the establishment of two Vietnams.

Despite Ho's purges of other nationalist groups, the Vietminh that defeated the French contained many noncommunist nationalists. Likewise, when North Vietnam was created all of the people were not hard-line communists like its leadership. "The majority of those Vietnamese who had supported the Vietminh resistance movement were attracted not by Marxism, but by non-Marxist and even anti-Marxist promises of democratic liberties and private ownership of land, and by appeals to patriotism."[32]

After the Geneva conference, changes were made in the objectives of the Northern leadership. Leaders from the North moved from the concept of "democratic revolution," which had appealed to the nationalists of the movement, to the more Marxist concept of "socialist revolution," which began to emphasize collectivization of society. This naturally caused strife, as results were occurring to people that they had not thought they had been fighting for. "Ho again emulated Stalin by launching a campaign to eliminate the *kulaks*—'landlords'—in his land reform campaign of 1955. Thousands were murdered and thousands more sent to Vietnamese gulags. In Ho's own province a revolt broke out against these excesses in November 1956. Ho's troops ruthlessly stamped out the revolt, and 6,000 peasants were killed or imprisoned."[33]

Many have wondered how many of these type uprisings occurred and were suppressed. This one, which was at Quyn Luu, occurred in the presence of the ICC, which was charged with the supervision of the 1954 Geneva Agreements. "The Quyn Luu uprising was the only popular revolt to receive publicity outside of North Vietnam, perhaps because of the presence of Canadian ICC representatives as witnesses, but it seemed to be only one of several disturbances."[34]

Needless to say, Ho Chi Minh prevailed. From 1956 to 1959 he consolidated his power and became ready for a new phase. Ho and the North would move from political to military struggle, this time in what had become South Vietnam. This phase would of course bring Ho into a collision course with the United States.

More recent history has tended to characterize Ho Chi Minh as a man who tended toward a combination of nationalism and communism. People have questioned as to whether he could have been an "Asian Tito." This view would liken Ho to the communist but fiercely nationalist and independent former leader of Yugoslavia. "Most available evidence, however does not support this analysis of Ho and his associates. The confusion has been caused by Vietnamese Communism's reliance upon nationalistic themes in the propaganda appeals for popular support, a practice which reflects less the Party's attitude toward 'nationalism' than the intense and widespread desire of the people for national independence from French colonialism."[35]

It has been mentioned earlier that after the Vietminh defeated the French at Dien Bien Phu and the Vietnamese had their own government in the North, goals and objectives changed. Nationalism was not a goal. Le Duan, first secretary of the Vietnamese Workers Party, asserted: "The communist and workers' parties have the obligation . . . to resolutely struggle against all manifestations of nationalism and chauvinism."[36]

Patriotism and nationalism had been acceptable sentiments prior to the victory over the French, but the post-1954 switch to the "socialist revolution" saw Ho Chi Minh redefining patriotism more to the international socialist mold. In 1951 he said, "Genuine patriotism is . . . part and parcel of internationalism."[37] Ho then said in 1956, "The Vietnam Workers Party . . . has proved that genuine patriotism can never be separated from proletarian internationalism."[38]

Ho Chi Minh died in 1969, but it can be assumed that his internationalist leanings lasted throughout his lifetime. This is apparent from this conclusion by Le Duan concerning Ho's last will and testament:

> On the basis of President Ho Chi Minh's last Testament, our party will work as energetically as it has in the past to restore and safeguard unity and cohesion within the socialist camp and among the fraternal parties on the basis of Marxism-Leninism and proletarian internationalism. We will continue to consolidate and tighten the unbreakable bonds of friendship between our country and the nations of the socialist camp, especially the Soviet Union and China. Cooperation and mutual assistance with the fraternal countries will be strengthened in all fields.[39]

In many instances Ho and his party seem to emphasize communist buzz words. *Socialist revolution* and *international proletarianism* are terms that occur in official renderings. It is assumed that proletarian internationalism implies subordination of nationalism and the nation-state to international working-class unity and world revolution. These are hardly the utterings of a fervent nationalist, yet they are used frequently by Ho and his comrades.

I hope this chapter has given the reader enough information concerning Ho Chi Minh to challenge his generally assumed nature as nationalist first and international communist second. It is also hoped that more knowledge about Ho in general will be gained. The question of Ho's nature serves as good background to the next chapter, which will examine the nature of the Vietnam War itself.

One view of Ho was personified by the antiwar activist Daniel Berrigan: "Ho Chi Minh even reminded Father Daniel Berrigan of Jesus Christ."[40] The other view of Ho has been espoused by William Stearnman of the School of Foreign Service at Georgetown University. He said, "Ho himself would have been absolutely appalled had he been called a nationalist by any other communist. He was one of the last international communists."[41]

Notes

1. John M. Blum, ed., *The National Experience, a History of the United States* (Forth Worth, TX: Harcourt, Brace, and Jovanovich, 1993), p. 803.
2. Carol Berkin et al., *American Voices, a History of the United States, 1865 to the Present* (Glenview, IL: Scott Foresman, 1995), p. 726.
3. Irwin Unger, *These United States, the Questions of Our Past* (Englewood Cliffs, NJ: Prentice Hall, 1995), p. 822.
4. Ibid., p. 842.
5. Ibid.
6. William Appleman Williams et al., *America in Vietnam, a Documentary History* (New York: Anchor Press/Doubleday, 1985), p. 97.
7. Paul Boyer, *Todd & Curti's The American Nation* (Austin, TX: Holt, Rhinehart, and Winston, 1995), p. 865.
8. Ibid.
9. Bernard Fall, *The Two Vietnams*, p. 235, as quoted in, Robert F. Turner, *Vietnamese Communism, Its Origins and Development* (Stanford, CA: Hoover Institution Publications, 1975), p. 8.

10. Joseph Buttinger, *Vietnam: A Dragon Embattled,* vol. 1 (New York: Frederick A. Praeger, 1967), p. 152.
11. Boyer, *The American Nation,* p. 866.
12. Harry G. Summers, Jr., *Vietnam War Almanac* (New York: Facts on File, 1985), p. 193.
13. Ibid.
14. *The Software Toolworks Multimedia Encyclopedia* (Novato, CA: Grolier, 1992).
15. Tony Murdoch, Joan M. Crouse, and Pam O'Connell, *Vietnam* (White Plains, NY: Longman, 1994), p. 12.
16. Robert F. Turner, *Vietnamese Communism, Its Origins and Development* (Stanford, CA: Hoover Institution Publications, 1975), p. 9.
17. P. J. Honey, ed., *North Vietnam Today,* p. 4, as quoted in ibid., p. 9.
18. Turner, *Vietnamese Communism,* pp. 9–10.
19. Ibid., p. 10.
20. Murdoch, Crouse, and O'Connell, *Vietnam,* p. 16.
21. David Halberstam, *Ho* (New York: Random House, 1971), p. 47.
22. Hoang Van Chi, *From Colonialism to Communism: A Case History of North Vietnam* (New York: Praeger, 1965), pp. 18–19.
23. Summers, *Vietnam War Almanac,* p. 193.
24. Ibid., pp. 193–94.
25. Ibid., p. 194.
26. George Donelson Moss, *Vietnam, an American Ordeal* (Englewood Cliffs, NJ: Prentice Hall, 1994), p. 28.
27. Turner, *Vietnamese Communism,* pp. 51–52.
28. Nguyen Phut Tan, *A Modern History of Vietnam,* p. 507, as quoted in ibid., p.53.
29. Neil Sheehan, *A Bright Shining Lie, John Paul Vann and America in Vietnam* (New York: Random House, 1988), p. 171.
30. Vo Nguyen Giap, *People's War, People's Army,* p.14 as quoted in Turner, *Vietnamese Communism,* p. 58.
31. Bernard Fall, in Giap, *People's War,* p. xxxi, as quoted in Turner, *Vietnamese Communism,* p. 58.
32. Turner, *Vietnamese Communism,* p.110.
33. Summers, *Vietnam War Almanac,* p. 194.
34. Turner, *Vietnamese Communism,* p. 166.
35. Ibid., p. 280.
36. Le Duan, *On Some Present International Problems,* p. 49, as quoted in Turner, *Vietnamese Communism,* p. 280.
37. Ho Chi Minh, *Selected Works,* 3:36, as quoted in Turner, *Vietnamese Communism,* p. 111.
38. Ho Chi Minh, *Selected Works,* 4:182, as quoted in Turner, *Vietnamese Communism.*

39. Le Duan, *The Vietnamese Revolution* (New York: International, 1971), p. 149.
40. Paul Hollander, *Political Pilgrims*, p. 374, as quoted in *Second Thoughts, Former Radicals Look Back at the Sixties* (New York: Madison, 1989), p. 247.
41. Willian Stearnman, videotape, *Television's Vietnam* (Washington, DC: Accuracy in Media, 1985).

6

The Nature of the War

During the Vietnam War and after, questions have been raised as to the nature of the war. Was the war a civil war or an invasion of the South by the North? The argument supporting the civil war thesis has been prefaced by the statement that after the Geneva Conference in 1954 there was to be an agreed-to reunification election held within two years. Support for the point of view that the United States and the South Vietnamese reneged on the agreement and therefore the communists in the North and South had no choice but to resort to force continues.

Differing points of view contend that for a variety of reasons after Geneva two separate nations, North and South Vietnam, came into existence. The logic that follows from this point of view is that the effort to reunify was then an invasion by the North of the South.

If, in fact, two nations were established during this time period, there are other slants on the civil war issue. The first slant would be that the war was an indigenous uprising of the South Vietnamese against South Vietnamese regimes that were basically neo-colonial puppets of the United States.

The counter to this slant is that there never was a truly indigenous Southern uprising but that the Southerners who did fight against the regime in the South were puppets (if you will) emanating from the North and/or trained, supported, and directed by the North Vietnamese.

These questions will be addressed in this chapter. The first step in dealing with these questions will be to return to an examination of the Geneva Conference in 1954 and analyze some information related to the conference. The conference, as the reader will recall, occurred after the French defeat at Dien Bien Phu and resulted in a division of Vietnam into North and South.

More recent high school textbooks do not directly state anything as to whether the war was a civil war or not. An earlier *Todd & Curti* edition did contain a statement concerning this issue. "Growing numbers of Americans were convinced that the Vietnam War was a grave mistake. They felt that the conflict was basically a civil war in which the United States should have no part."[1]

Three high school textbooks give the distinct impression that it was the United States and the regime of Ngo Dinh Diem that were solely responsible for the demise of the reunification elections. It then can be concluded that the perpetuation of the division of Vietnam and hence the war can be attributed to these parties.

American Voices, a History of the United States puts it this way: "Realizing that the Vietminh would likely win any election in Vietnam, the United States did not sign the Geneva Accords. . . . Diem refused to permit the promised elections. Instead he set out to consolidate his power in the diverse and factionalized new nation of South Vietnam."[2]

Todd & Curti's The American Nation addresses the issue this way: "General elections to reunify the country were scheduled for July 1956. Alarmed that the Communists would likely win a nationwide election, the United States refused to endorse the agreement."[3]

Finally the textbook *The National Experience, a History of the United States* brings in Diem, SEATO, and the U.S. administration. "After setting up SEATO, the administration now backed South Vietnam's new premier, Ngo Dinh Diem, a devout Catholic and stubborn nationalist whose strength of purpose had impressed many Americans, liberal and conservative. Diem rejected the elections provided for in the Geneva Accords."[4]

The limited information in these high school textbooks could and most likely would lead to erroneous conclusions. Among these conclusions would be that the United States was opposed to democratic elections in Vietnam and totally opposed the provisions of the Geneva Accords. It also could be concluded that Diem in South Vietnam was opposed to democratic elections in Vietnam.

It does need to be remembered that neither the United States nor South Vietnam signed the Geneva Accords so therefore were not necessarily bound by them. Having said that, it is also necessary to note in reference to the Geneva Armistice and Accords that "the armistice agreement was reached over the objection of South Vietnam, which did not sign it. The South Vietnamese also objected to the terms of the Final Agreement, which had been unilaterally agreed to by the French without prior consultation with the South Vietnamese delegates to the conference."[5]

The United States, for its part, did not concur with the Geneva agreements totally. The U.S position was that it "pledged that it would refrain from use of force or the threat of force to disturb their provisions."[6]

When it comes to the issue of elections there are a few items that need clarification. First, the United States was not against free democratic elections. In the same document that the United States made the previous pledge to not disturb the provisions of the Geneva Accords, Undersecretary of State Walter Bedell Smith also stated: "In the case of nations now divided against their will, we shall continue to seek to achieve unity through free elections supervised by the United Nations to insure that they are conducted fairly."[7]

As for the attitude of the South Vietnamese concerning free unification elections:

> The Diem government continued to support the concept of re-unification elections, but insisted that they be supervised by the United Nations. Diem argued that genuinely free elections would be impossible without adequate supervision, since a majority of the population lived in the North under a totalitarian Communist regime. The ICC was unacceptable to him because of the veto power of a Communist state, Poland. The Ho Chi Minh regime was unwilling to agree to United Nations supervision.[8]

After the 1954 defeat of the French, Communist Party cadres in the South were anxious to be regrouped and sent to the North as the Geneva agreements had stated. They were not, however, allowed to go to the North but told to stay in the South to work as underground agents. "In order to win the general election, the communist party had a scheme to plant its agents as underground workers in South Vietnam."[9]

It is easy to see that the simplistic explanations could lead to simplistic conclusions concerning the pivotal events of 1954–56 and the reunification elections. It appears that far from reneging on the elections, provided for in the accords that the United States and South Vietnamese did not even sign, that the U.S. and the South Vietnamese welcomed elections under supervision of the United Nations. It was the North Vietnamese who shunned UN supervision of what possibly could have been truly free elections. Given Ho Chi Minh's track record in dealing with domestic opposition, it does not seem very likely that truly free elections would have occurred.

There are other matters and evidence surrounding the Geneva Conference that place into doubt if reunification elections were ever really expected by the Geneva signatories to succeed. These doubts were even shared by the North Vietnamese themselves. Victor Bator argues: "It appears obvious that the unification of Vietnam—foreseen in paragraph 7 of the Final Declaration and to be achieved by a referendum-type election in July, 1956, two years after Geneva—could not have been seriously contemplated."[10]

Further support for this point of view comes from P. J. Honey, a British scholar who quoted chief Vietminh negotiator Pham Van Dong as saying "You know as well as I do that there won't be any elections."[11]

In more recent history the Chinese views on reunification have come to light and allow some insight as to the reality of the possibility of elections. A 1983 Fox Butterfield article in the *New York Times Magazine* stated: "Vietnam's leaders now claim that the Chinese actually cut off military aid to them in 1954 to compel them to negotiate with the French and accept the division of the country. . . . And several scholars have found records indicating that Zhou Enlai, China's prime minister, expected the separation of Vietnam to be long-lasting and turned down Ho's request in 1956 for help in arranging the elections."[12]

Another argument concerning the demise of the elections for reunification of Vietnam is that the Geneva Accords themselves were vague and weak and never strongly supported even by the signatories. "The conclusion at Geneva was to be misinterpreted, if not misunderstood, for years to come. The only documents signed were cease-fire accords ending the hostilities in Vietnam."[13] The agreements were, as explained earlier (chapter 2), an incoherent manifesto, a hodgepodge of pseudo-agreements in the first place.

The following discusses whether the intent of the Geneva Accords was to lead to the future reunification of Vietnam:

But what needs to be pointed out is that the accords themselves did not further that intent. By creating two regimes responsible for "civil administration" . . . by providing for the regroupment of forces to two zones and by putting off national elections for two years, the conferees had actually made a future political settlement for Vietnam extremely unlikely. . . . Thus, the call for elections in the Final Declaration had as little a chance of implementation in Vietnam as previously in Korea and Germany, a point brought home by Vietnamese officials and reinforced by the failure of the same Geneva conferees to agree on a political settlement in Korea. . . . If the intent of the Geneva accords was subverted, the subverters were the conferees themselves, who aspired to an ideal political settlement incompatible with the physical and psychological dismemberment of Vietnam on July 21, 1954.[14]

It should be clear at this point that there were many factors that caused the reunification elections for Vietnam to not occur. Straight-line thinking that U.S. actions to stymie the reunification elections alone led to inevitable war in Vietnam is gross oversimplification even if at times it appears to be the mainstream thought.

The issue of whether the war was a civil war led by indigenous South Vietnamese revolting against the South Vietnamese government necessitates a discussion of the nature of the NLF. This discussion needs to include its origin, its platform, and its status during the course of and after the Vietnam War.

Whatever its origin, which is a debatable point, the NLF came into existence on December 20, 1960. Excerpts of its manifesto will be listed here. Later in this chapter an examination of the consistency of what the NLF stated as its goals and what happened in South Vietnam in 1975 will occur. Readers will then be able to form their own conclusions relating to some issues that are being raised in this chapter.

Excerpts from the *Manifesto of the South Vietnam National Front for Liberation* follow:

The South Vietnam Front for Liberation undertakes to unite all sections of the people, all social classes, nationalities, political parties, organizations, religious communities and patriotic personalities, without distinction of their political tendencies, in order to struggle for the overthrow of the rule of the U.S. imperialists and their stooges—Ngo Dinh Diem clique—and for the realization of independence, peace and *neutrality* pending the peaceful reunification of the fatherland.[15]

Other excerpts from the NLF manifesto include:

2. To bring into being a broad and progressive democracy, promulgate freedom of expression, of the press, of belief, of assembly, of association, of movement and other democratic freedoms . . .
    9. To re-establish normal relations between the two zones, pending peaceful reunification of the fatherland.[16]

At a later date in 1965 the NLF included in their platform with the *Statement of the South Viet Nam N.L.F. Central Committee concerning Intensification/Expansion of the U.S. War* this excerpt: "2. The heroic People of South Viet Nam are resolved to drive out the U.S. imperialists in order to liberate themselves and achieve an independent, democratic, peaceful and neutral South Viet Nam, pending national reunification."[17]

Clearly in both statements there was an emphasis that there would be a peaceful reunification of North and South. The Southerners appear to imply that there will be an independent South Vietnam under different auspices that will voluntarily reunify with the North.

Before going any further in analyzing these matters the characterization of the NLF by high school textbooks will be ex-

110

amined. The first textbook examined will be *The National Experience, a History of the United States*. It states: "In 1958 A Communist-nationalist movement called the National Liberation Front or, more popularly, the Vietcong began guerrilla warfare against Diem."[18] While very brief, the coverage of the NLF concludes that both communists and nationalists were in the movement.

Todd & Curti's The American Nation gives more extensive coverage to the NLF. It says:

> By the late 1950s armed revolution had erupted in the south. In 1959, military assistance began flowing from the north to the Vietminh who had stayed in the south. In 1960 the southern Vietminh formed the National Liberation Front (NLF). The NLF's main goal was to overthrow the Ngo Dinh Diem regime. Members of this rebel force were called Vietcong (Vietnamese Communists) by their opponents, but not all NLF supporters were Communists.[19]

This text emphasized that all NLF members were not communists. It also stated that the NLF's main goal was the overthrow of the Diem regime. By these two statements support is given to the civil war, indigenous revolt thesis. There is mention of military assistance from the North, but it could be concluded that there was not an expansionist communist element as a driving force of the NLF.

The textbook *American Voices, a History of the United States 1865 to the Present* addresses the NLF in this fashion: "Ho had left many reunification supporters behind in the south when the nation was partitioned in 1954. They remained ready to revive the struggle. . . . By 1958 forces loyal to Ho had launched a new civil war in the South, encouraged and supplied by Hanoi. In 1960 they organized the National Front for

111

the Liberation of Vietnam (NLF), known to its opponents as the Viet Cong, or Vietnamese communists."[20]

This text points out that it was forces loyal to the North and Ho that revived the struggle that would support the Northern invasion thesis. It also labels the war a civil war, which of course supports the civil war thesis even though the concept of indigenous Southerners is in doubt.

The last textbook examined, *These United States, the Questions of Our Past,* puts it this way: "Diem and his supporters proved corrupt and unpopular with the country's Buddhists and peasantry and before long the Vietcong (called by its friends the National Liberation Front), a Communist guerrilla movement supplied with arms by Ho Chi Minh in North Vietnam, began to attract a following among the rural people."[21] This text implies that the war was an uprising of native Southern rural peasants and Buddhists.

For the most part the high school textbooks leave the issue of the origins of the NLF somewhat cloudy. The textbooks do lean toward the implication that the war was basically an indigenous Southern revolt by nationalists and communists who were fighting the evil Diem regime. Help from the North is alluded to, but the North is **not** cited as the prime motivating force behind the formation of the NLF.

Mainstream academia during and after the war basically took the position of the most influential account of the origins of the NLF. This position was advanced by two Cornell professors, George McT. Kahin and John W. Lewis, in the book *The United States in Vietnam.* In this book the authors argued that the Vietcong were "Southern rooted."[22]

Kahlin and Lewis contend that the communists withdrew all their armed forces to the newly created North Vietnam and left behind only political cadres. The argument goes on to say that Hanoi favored only political, not armed, struggle, but the harshness and heavy-handedness of the Diem regime caused

112

the Southerners to lose patience with the North and organize an insurgency led by the NLF. Hanoi then reluctantly was obligated to sanction the Southerners' actions. Another conclusion by the professors was that there was no evidence that Hanoi directed the formation of the NLF.[23]

A book directed at young people and published in 1993 supports the previous conclusion made by the Cornell professors. In *Three Faces of Vietnam,* author Richard L. Wormser writes: "But the Vietminh, the South Vietnamese communists, now called Vietcong by Diem, were forced to take matters into their own hands. . . . Ho finally had to approve their struggle."[24]

Another book directed at young people, *The Vietnam War Opposing Viewpoints,* has an article in it by Joseph A. Amter that offers support for the indigenous Southern peasant rebellion thesis. Citing the corruptness and ruthlessness of the Diem regime, the author states: "In reaction, the peasants formed a rebel organization, the National Liberation Front, together with a loosely organized guerrilla army known as the Vietcong."[25]

Mainstream academia and others have accepted and promoted the foregoing explanation of the origin of the NLF. Other sources more recently have exposed another and differing side to the story concerning the NLF's beginnings.

The other side of the story begins with: "But a history published by the People's Army of Vietnam in 1980 titled 'The Anti-U.S. Resistance War for National Salvation, 1954–1975: Military Events' contends that Hanoi played a large role in the development of the Vietcong."[26] The next passage was written and cited earlier in this book (chapter 2) and is repeated here: "When the N.L.F. was proclaimed, this official Communist history goes on, it was done at the order of the party in Hanoi, and the Front's program 'followed the line delineated by our party.'"

A last passage can be used as the concluding comment on the origins of the NLF. "After the war the North Vietnamese freely admitted that the NLF was their own creation, totally controlled and directed from Hanoi."[27] This passage and the others certainly attack the indigenous civil war thesis and lend credibility to the Northern invasion thesis.

Discussion of the nature of the war necessitates an examination of the role of the North Vietnamese army in it. Certain questions need to be discussed relating to their involvement. When did they first send troops south? Were their troops a response to U.S. escalation? How many troops were sent south? What role did the North Vietnamese Army (NVA) regulars play in the war vis-à-vis the South Vietnamese Vietcong? These and other questions will be discussed.

An earlier version of a high school textbook by Todd & Curti, *Triumph of the American Nation* implies that North Vietnamese involvement in the war was in response to U.S. escalation. The book relates that the United States began bombing the North in 1965. It then describes the U.S. troop buildup from 1965 to 1967 and states: "As American aid increased, North Vietnam increased its support of the Vietcong. . . . As the war went on, troops from North Vietnam also moved south, along the trail to join the Vietcong in the fighting."[28]

In a later textbook, *Todd & Curti's The American Nation*, it was written in reference to the February 1965 bombing campaign, Rolling Thunder: "Although the air war was designed to bring U.S. involvement in Vietnam quickly to an end, it had the opposite effect: North Vietnam—rather than surrendering—sent more troops and supplies south."[29] The same logic that it was U.S. escalation that led to North Vietnamese participation is used in this textbook.

Similar logic is used in the textbook *The National Experience: A History of the United States*: "Hanoi had meantime sent men into South Vietnam—4,400 to 7,400 in 1964, according to American estimates, and mostly native southerners. Now, in response to American escalation, units of North Vietnamese regular army began for the first time to appear in South Vietnam."[30] This passage's referral to "native southerners" supports the indigenous civil war thesis and repeats the argument that NVA participation resulted from American escalation.

Contrary to the way it has been depicted or alluded to in these textbooks, it was NVA regulars who had been infiltrating into the South long before U.S. escalation or bombing. It has been cited elsewhere in this book (chapter 4) that the North had at least three regiments, totalling over five thousand men, in the South by March of 1965, when the bombing began. North Vietnam had introduced combat forces into the South well before U.S. bombing or U.S. combat troops. "Washington had long maintained that Hanoi started infiltrating its regular army units in the fall of 1964, prompting President Johnson's decision to begin bombing North Vietnam and then to dispatch American ground forces to South Vietnam a few months earlier."[31]

North Vietnam up until the end of the war denied that it even had troops in the South. "When I visited North Vietnam in 1969, Prime Minister Pham Van Dong said it with a straight face that there were no Northern troops in the South."[32] "The reason for this pretense was that the communists needed to represent the insurgency against Diem as an internal South Vietnamese rebellion—a civil war rather than an invasion from the North—just as they needed a front organization like the NLF to conceal the fact that they were in control."[33]

More basically, the argument over the issue of North Vietnamese regulars in the South diverts attention from the larger pattern of North Vietnamese intervention, which, as we have seen, goes back to at least 1959. Contrary to communist propaganda, the southern insurgency was never a spontaneous uprising but from the beginning was a deliberate campaign, directed and supported from Hanoi. In view of the extensive involvement of North Vietnam, it was also misplaced to regard the conflict as simply a "civil war."[34]

It became clear as the war progressed that if it had once been primarily a South Vietnamese affair it did not continue to be so. Increasing numbers of North Vietnamese continued to infiltrate. In 1965 there were 60,000 NVA troops in the South. From 1965 onward an estimated 5,000 to 6,000 NVA troops were sent to the South as replacement and reinforcements until by 1967 there were 200,000 NVA troops in South Vietnam.[35]

In January of 1968 the communists launched the Tet Offensive (to be addressed more in a later chapter), in which the NLF and Vietcong cadres were decimated. Some assert that the North sent the Vietcong on this offensive and knew they would be destroyed, thereby eliminating the Southerners as rivals for power in any unified Vietnam that might come into being in the future. "From that point on, North Vietnamese troops did 80 percent of the fighting in the South and the war could no longer be represented as an internal insurgency or a 'people's' war."[36]

In 1972 the NLF's political and military apparatus remained weak. This is attested to by the fact that the 1972 communist offensive, which also was defeated, was spearheaded by at least fourteen North Vietnamese divisions. Richard Nixon commented on this offensive by saying: "There was no credible way for Hanoi to claim any longer that the war in the South was a civil war between the Saigon government and the Vietcong, so North Vietnam dropped the facade of 'civil war' and launched a full-scale conventional invasion of the South."[37]

The Northerners continued to increase their dominance after U.S. forces left in 1973. The fall of Saigon in 1975 can be accurately called a conquest by the North. It was predominantly the NVA that surrounded Saigon and forced the South

Vietnamese government to surrender. "Indeed, the Communists had lost the 'peoples war,' and the war they finally won was a conventional war fought by regular uniformed troops equipped with tanks and planes and missiles, not an insurgency fought by primitively armed guerrillas in black pajamas."[38] This war was won by invaders from the North.

Contrast this research to the myth that continues to be perpetuated in some quarters, either by accident or by conscious effort, to freeze historical understanding in the mistaken interpretations of the past. *Time Magazine* publishes and circulates a teaching guide for its education program. This guide accompanies classroom use of the magazine. In the April 24, 1995, guide there is a chart containing a chronology of the Vietnam War. The guide has identified 1957 as the year that communist guerrillas, known as the Vietcong, began attacks on South Vietnam. The guide states that in 1975, "in late April, South Vietnam falls to the Vietcong."[39] As noted, South Vietnam did not fall to the Vietcong, which *Time* previously labeled as "Communist guerrillas," but to the NVA. *Time* has been informed of the error, and no correction has been forthcoming.

Phillip Davidson Jr., who was chief intelligence officer in Vietnam, had this to say about the nature of the war in Vietnam: "First the Vietnam war was *not* a civil war, nor a South Vietnamese insurgency. . . . From 1964, when the first North Vietnamese entered South Vietnam, until 1975, the war was an outright invasion of South Vietnam by North Vietnam."[40] G. Gordon Liddy emphatically stated it this way: "The Vietnam War was *not* a 'civil war.' It was aggression by one state, valid politically and having ethnically different people, against another such state."[41]

Events following the end of the war support the argument that the war was an invasion rather than a civil war. To examine this subject it is necessary to look back at what was said prior to the war by the NLF and North Vietnam. Scenarios of what

117

was supposed to occur as opposed to what actually occurred will be contrasted.

Portions of the manifesto of the NLF as has been related earlier in this chapter stated that the Southerners expected that South Vietnam would be a somewhat of a separate entity and reunification with the North would be a slow, negotiated process between the two zones after military success had been achieved. Evidence will show that given what had been enunciated, this conclusion by the South was logical.

The Provisional Revolutionary Government (PRG), which was established in 1969, was the Southern revolutionaries' alternative government. It was very similar to the NLF but was attempting to be somewhat of a shadow government to the government of the Republic of South Vietnam. The PRG's goal was to present itself as equally legitimate to the existing government to the people of the South as well as the rest of the world. The PRG stated that it stood "for the formation of a provisional coalition government based on the principle of equality, democracy, and mutual respect."[42] This organization called for a government of the South that included communists, anticommunists, and neutralists in a coalition.

In reference to unification of North and South the PRG desired to reestablish normal relations between the South and North and stated: "The unification of the country will be achieved step by step through peaceful methods and on the basis of discussions and agreement between both zones, without coercion by either side."[43] It is clear that the PRG's desires reflect the same concept that the NLF had of a reunification that was to be slowly negotiated by the two zones. The Southerners seemed to have envisioned a confederation or partnership with the North. When the war concluded in 1975 some of the Southerners had apparently envisioned an independent South Vietnam. "South Vietnam, at about this time, was seeking United Nations representation separately from North Vietnam."[44]

Southern sentiments concerning these matters were reinforced in the early going in the struggle by pronouncements coming from the North.

> Such reasons were easy enough to come by. In the first place, they had heard for years the solemnly proclaimed avowals of the DRV that the South was "a special and unique situation, very different from the North." "The South," said Le Duan, Party secretary general, "needs its own policy." "Construct Socialism in the North," rang the slogan. "Develop the National Democratic Revolution in the South." "No one," as Pham Van Dong (DRV prime minister) liked to declare to his Western visitors, "has the stupid and criminal idea of annexing the South." Over the years, such statements, persistently and fervently reiterated in broadcasts, manifestos, and even in internal Party documents, had had their effect.[45]

"How could we have the stupid, criminal idea of annexing the South?" said Pham Van Dong to various foreign visitors. "We have no wish to impose communism on the South," said Le Duc Tho to the international press in Paris."[46] These sentiments obviously fell on believing ears in the international community as well as within the NLF and the PRG.

The defeat and surrender of the South Vietnamese government in 1975, accomplished mainly by the North Vietnamese, changed the whole scenario in the South. What had been envisioned by the Southerners as occurring after the struggle rapidly disappeared as the Northern conquerors seemingly changed their avowed beliefs concerning the future of the South and the role of the Southerners. The actions of the Northerners resembled more of a military conquest by them than a joint effort with the rebellious Southerners to wrest power from an illegitimate South Vietnamese government.

Unification was achieved unilaterally without meaningful input by the Southerners. Power positions in the government went almost exclusively to Northerners who proceeded to rule the South.

> Since the war, some members of the N.L.F. have contended they themselves had been deceived by Hanoi. Writing last fall in *The New York Review of Books,* Troung Nhu Tang, the former Minister of Justice in the N.L.F.'s government and a French educated "independent socialist," indicated that he joined the Vietcong because he believed the Communists' promises that they would work for an autonomous, democratic South. At the end of the war, Hanoi annexed the South and the N.L.F. was disbanded.
>
> At "the simple farewell dinner" held to disband the N.L.F. in 1976, Mr. Tang recalled, neither the party nor the Government bothered to send a representative. "I was tragically wrong" about the Communists, he wrote. "The North Vietnamese Communists, survivors of protracted, blood-drenched campaigns against colonialism, interventionism and human oppression, became in their turn colonialists, interventionists and architects of one of the world's most rigid regimes."[47]

Doan Van Toai, an intelligence agent for the NLF and a leader of student demonstrations against the Thieu regime and U.S. involvement, revealed the relegation of the NLF to an almost nonexistent role in the governance of the newly liberated Vietnam. In 1981 he wrote: "Today, among 17 members of the Politburo and 134 members of the Vietnamese Communist Party, not a single one is from the NLF."[48] The North muscled out not only the nationalist element of the South but the communists as well.

The duplicity of the North in this process is now unashamedly admitted by them. A Northern party historian stated it this way: "The Provisional Revolutionary Government was always simply a group emanating from the DRV. If we [the] DRV had pretended otherwise for such a long time, it was only because during the war we were not obliged to reveal our cards."[49]

The North had total power in their hands after the military defeat of the South. With this total power they made it understood that the Vietnam of the future would be a single monolithic bloc, collectivist and totalitarian. The traditions and culture of the South would be molded by the Northern political machine as conquerors. By this time they proceeded to install themselves into the positions of power without concern for the niceties of appearance.[50]

> The PRG and the National Liberation Front, whose programs had embodied the desire of so many South Vietnamese to achieve a political solution to their troubles and reconciliation among a people devastated by three decades of civil war—this movement the Northern Party had considered all along as simply the last linkup it needed to achieve its own imperialistic revolution. After the 1975 victory, the Front and PRG not only had no further role to play; they became a positive obstacle to the rapid consolidation of power.[51]

Dr. Duong Quynh Hoa was the minister of health for the PRG. Dr. Hoa was named a heroine of the revolution after the defeat of the Saigon regime. She was also, as deputy minister of health, one of the few Southerners who were given a position of importance after the war. She became so disillusioned with the party and the second-rate people running things in the South that she left the party, government, and politics. Her views on the North were expressed in a discussion with CBS News commentator Morley Safer: "Dr. Hoa tells me that the Northerners are regarded as another invader, another usurper."[52]

Events that had transpired are summed up in a story related by Troung Nhu Tang (the former PRG minister of justice).

121

Tang was in Hanoi during the liberation of Saigon in 1975. While there he spent some time with Truong Chinh, who was a member and theoretician of the Politburo (ruling group) of North Vietnam and then the unified Vietnam. On the night of liberation a banquet was given in Hanoi in honor of the Southern leadership, attended by most of the high-ranking North Vietnamese officials.

Fifteen months later Tang (the Southerner) met Chinh (the Northerner) at a conference for the formal ratification of the unification of the North and the South. Tang relates this conversation beginning with Chinh speaking to Tang: " 'Excuse me, comrade,' he said. 'You look familiar to me. Who are you again?' For a moment I was nonplussed—to say the least. When I answered that I was the minister of justice for the South, Chinh's eyes lit up. 'Oh really?' he said. 'What's your name, and what are you doing now?'"[53]

At this point the reader, given the information in this chapter as contrasted to traditional utterings concerning the nature of the Vietnam War, should be better able to make a judgment concerning its nature. Was it an indigenous civil war or was it an invasion and conquest of South Vietnam by the North?

Notes

1. Lewis Paul Todd and Merle Curti, *Triumph of the American Nation* (Orlando, FL: Harcourt, Brace, and Jovanovich, 1986), p. 922.
2. Carol Berkin et al., *American Voices, a History of the United States, 1865 to the Present* (Glenview, IL: Scott Foresman, 1995), p. 727.
3. Paul Boyer, *Todd & Curti's The American Nation* (Austin, TX: Holt, Rhinehart, and Winston, 1995), p. 868.
4. John M. Blum, ed., *The National Experience, a History of the United States* (Fort Worth, TX: Harcourt, Brace, and Jovanovich, 1993), p. 818.
5. Harry G. Summers, Jr., *Vietnam War Almanac* (New York: Facts on File, 1985), p. 177.

6. Ibid.
7. United States Senate, Committee on Foreign Relations, *Information Relating to Southeast Asia and Vietnam*, 90th Congress, 1st Session (Washington, D.C., 1967), p. 83, quoted in William Appleman Williams et al., *America in Vietnam, a Documentary History (New York: Anchor Press/Doubleday, 1985), p. 170*.
8. Robert F. Turner, *Vietnamese Communism, Its Origins and Development* (Stanford, CA: Hoover Institution Publications, 1975), p. 107.
9. Nguyen Van Canh, *Vietnam under Communism 1975–1982* (Stanford, CA: Hoover Institution Press, 1983), p. 7.
10. Victor Bator, *Vietnam, a Diplomatic Tragedy*, p. 129, as quoted in Turner, *Vietnamese Communism*, p. 107.
11. P. J. Honey, *Communism in North Vietnam*, p. 6, as quoted in Turner, *Vietnamese Communism*, p. 107.
12. Fox Butterfield, "The New Vietnam Scholarship," *New York Times Magazine*, February 13, 1983, p. 31.
13. Stanley Karnow, *Vietnam, a History, the First Complete Account of Vietnam at War* (New York: Penguin, 1983), p. 204.
14. *Pentagon Papers*, pp. 165–66, as quoted in Turner, *Vietnamese Communism*, p. 108.
15. *South Viet Nam National Front for Liberation, Documents* (Vietnam: Gia Phong, 1968), pp. 11–18, as quoted in *Vietnam, a Visual Investigation* (CD-ROM) (Redmond, WA: Medio Multimedia, 1994).
16. Ibid.
17. Ibid., pp. 33–52.
18. Blum, *The National Experience*, p. 818.
19. Boyer, *The American Nation*, p. 868.
20. Berkin et al., *American Voices*, p. 726.
21. Irwin Unger, *These United States, the Questions of Our Past* (Englewood Cliffs, NJ: Prentice Hall, 1995), p. 822.
22. Butterfield, "The New Vietnam Scholarship," p. 31.
23. Ibid.
24. Richard L. Wormser, *Three Faces of Vietnam* (New York: Franklin Watts, 1993), p. 41.
25. Joseph A. Amter, reprinted in David L. Bender, *The Vietnam War Opposing Viewpoints* (St. Paul, MN: Greenhaven, 1984), p. 127.
26. Butterfield, "The New Vietnam Scholarship," p. 32.
27. Summers, *Vietnam War Almanac*, p. 259.
28. Lewis Paul Todd and Merle Curti, *Triumph of the American Nation* (Orlando, FL: Harcourt, Brace, Jovanovich, 1986), p. 922.
29. Boyer, *The American Nation*, p. 873.
30. Blum, *The National Experience*, p. 849.
31. Butterfield, "The New Vietnam Scholarship," p. 32.
32. Ibid.

33. Norman Podhoretz, *Why We Were in Vietnam* (New York: Simon and Schuster, 1982), p. 44.
34. Guenter Lewy, *American in Vietnam* (New York: Oxford University Press, 1978), p. 40.
35. Canh, *Vietnam under Communism,* p. 10.
36. Podhoretz, *Why We Were in Vietnam,* p. 172.
37. Richard Nixon, *The Real War* (New York: Warner, 1980), p. 112.
38. Podhoretz, *Why We Were in Vietnam,* p. 172.
39. *Time Education Program Teachers Guide, Time Magazine,* April 24, 1995.
40. Bill McCloud, *What We Should Tell Our Children about Vietnam* (Norman: University of Oklahoma Press, 1989), pp. 32–33.
41. Ibid., p. 75.
42. *Action Program of the Provisional Revolutionary Government of the Republic of South Vietnam,* as quoted in Troung Nhu Tang, *A Vietcong Memoir* (New York: Vintages, 1985), p. 336.
43. Tang, *A Vietcong Memoir,* p. 338.
44. JOAK TV, Tokyo, "Interview with Wilfred Burchett by NHK Correspondent Nagata," *News Center Nine O'Clock* (Program), September 19, 1975, JPRS, no. 65867; *Vietnam,* no. 1711, October 7, 1975, pp. 40–41, as quoted in Canh, *Vietnam under Communism,* p. 19.
45. Tang, *A Vietcong Memoir,* p. 135.
46. Ibid.
47. Butterfield, "The New Vietnam Scholarship," p. 35.
48. Doan Van Toai, "A Lament for Vietnam," *New York Times Magazine,* March 29, 1881, quoted in Podhoretz, *Why We Were in Vietnam,* p. 175.
49. Tang, *A Vietnam Memoir,* p. 268.
50. Ibid.
51. Ibid.
52. Morley Safer, *Flashbacks on Returning to Vietnam* (New York: Random House, 1990), p. 42.
53. Tang, *A Vietnam Memoir,* p. 286.

7

The Tet Offensive—Victory into Defeat

Any comprehensive work about the Vietnam War would be incomplete without a discussion of the Tet Offensive. This offensive may have been **the** pivotal event of the Vietnam War as far as U.S. involvement was concerned.

Tet is also somewhat of a mystery. As Col. Harry G. Summers has said, "One of the great mysteries of the Vietnam War is how the allied military victory during the Tet Offensive, a victory so complete that for the rest of the war the Vietcong guerrillas never again played a significant military role, ultimately was turned into an American political defeat."[1]

Added to the mystery is a description of uniqueness. It has been said that the Tet Offensive was "probably unique in that the side that lost completely in the tactical sense came away with a psychological and hence a political victory."[2]

As has been related earlier in this book (chapter 4), the Tet Offensive was launched by the communists in late January of 1968 during an agreed-upon cease-fire for the Vietnamese holiday celebrating the lunar New Year. The offensive achieved initial success but was eventually repulsed by U.S. and South Vietnamese forces who inflicted massive damage on enemy forces. Unfortunately for the allied side, the military victory was perceived as a defeat in the United States and is suspected of turning U.S. public opinion irreversibly toward a more negative attitude concerning the U.S. effort in Vietnam. This chapter will give more in-depth analysis of the Tet Offensive and will attempt to expose the reader to a broader perspective of this pivotal event.

An objective examination of the Tet Offensive should include first what are believed to have been the enemy's objectives for the offensive. After that, an assessment of whether these objectives were met would generally be a fair assessment of the success of the offensive.

Overwhelming evidence indicates that it was the major goal of the communists to have what was called a "general uprising" of the South Vietnamese people against the South Vietnamese government. "In their internal discussions at lower levels there is considerable evidence that the Communists actually expected the people of South Vietnam to rise up and join them in overthrowing the government of South Vietnam."[3] Not only did the South Vietnamese communists have this optimistic goal, but the North Vietnamese rank-and-file soldiers held the same view. "North Vietnamese Army soldiers who infiltrated South to participate in the attacks report that they were told that this would be the last battle of the war, and that the people were prepared to follow them to victory."[4] This optimism originated from the Lao Dong (Communist Central Committee in the North). "The Central Committee strongly believed that the time was now ripe for a bold and closely coordinated decisive onslaught that would inspire the people to a mass uprising, topple the South Vietnamese 'lackeys' and win the war quickly by forcing the 'imperialist' aggressors to lose heart and retreat from Southeast Asia forever."[5]

The general uprising was to occur after the communists seized key urban areas, especially Saigon, the capital of the South. Military objectives throughout history have generally included the seizure of the enemy's capital city. "The People would then wrest control of the cities and villages from Saigon control, bring down the national assembly and achieve Communist mastery over the countryside."[6]

Gen. William Westmoreland, commander of U.S. forces in Vietnam at the time, offers a differing version of communist strategy for Tet. Westmoreland's thesis was that the country-wide attacks in South Vietnam were a diversion for other major plans: "The most logical course for the enemy, it seemed to me was to make a strong effort to overrun the two northern provinces while at the same time launching lesser attacks throughout the country to try to tie down American forces that might be moved to reinforce northern South Vietnam, the most vulnerable part of the country."[7] Westmoreland further explained: "But the climactic battle of the Tet Offensive was at Khe Sanh in Quang Tri province. As at Dien Bien Phu fourteen years earlier, North Vietnamese General Vo Nguyen Giap hoped not only to gain a tactical military victory. He hoped to inflict a catastrophic 'Dien Bien Phu' during an American election year and with the seizure of the two northern provinces gain leverage with which to go to the negotiating table."[8]

Departing from debate as to what the communists' priorities were during Tet, the various goals set forth can be summarized. They intended to coordinate numerous attacks taking urban areas including the capital of Saigon. This would cause the South Vietnamese to have a general uprising and overthrow the South Vietnamese government. Alternatively the strategy may have intended to make a "Dien Bien Phu" out of Khe Sanh and seize the two northernmost provinces in South Vietnam as a prelude to opening negotiations.

None of these goals were met by the communists. They took but were not able to hold urban areas. The general uprising did not occur. They also did not take Khe Sanh or the two northern provinces.

The results of Tet were by any objective analysis a disaster for the North Vietnamese and especially their allies the Vietcong. "Nothing remotely resembling a General Uprising occurred. . . . Except at Hue and Khe Sanh, most of the combat that could be considered part of the Tet Offensive was over by February 11, a fortnight after it began. All towns and cities of the two northern provinces had been cleared."[9]

Tet proved to be a disaster militarily for communist forces, as the various statements that follow will assert: "Enemy losses have been heavy; he has failed to achieve his prime objectives of mass uprisings and capture of a large number of the capital cities and towns. Morale in enemy units which were badly mauled or where the men were oversold the idea of a decisive victory at TET probably has suffered severely."[10] "In the Tet Offensive only, the losses on the battlefield were estimated at 70,000 men."[11] Nguyen Van Canh, a South Vietnamese law professor and author, said of the long-range results of Tet: "From the Tet Offensive to October 31, 1970, it was estimated that the communist forces lost 515,000 men, including 44,000 political cadres at the chapter and village levels and some 90,000 defectors. In interviews with defectors the author learned that by the end of 1968, there were only some four hundred seriously depleted party chapters in all South Vietnam."[12] "Mr. Tang, the former N.L.F. Minister of Justice, has described Tet as 'catastrophic'; he calculated the Vietcong lost half their forces and new recruits could not be found locally to replace them."[13] Vietnam scholar and college political science professor Samuel L. Popkin said in reference to Tet that it "totally destroyed the idea of the inevitability of an N.L.F. victory in the villages. When the villagers saw the stacks of Vietcong bodies in Saigon on their local TV sets, they rushed to get their sons into local defense forces."[14] They did this so that their sons wouldn't be drafted by the Vietcong.

Robert Turner has written: "On the negative side of the political balance sheet within South Vietnam, the Tet Offensive was in many areas disastrous for the Communist infrastructure (VCI). . . . Even more important, in areas where the VCI had been compromised the Party was left with little or no organiza-

128

tion. It had taken many years to establish the VCI, and its loss was to have a serious effect on Communist capabilities during the years which followed."[15]

The consensus of opinion from many other quarters supports the view that the Tet Offensive was a tactical and military disaster for the communist side. Dr. Duong Quynh Hoa, a prominent communist figure during the war, told Stanley Karnow, "We lost our best people."[16] "In retrospect, she bluntly denounced the venture as a 'grievous miscalculation' by the Hanoi hierarchy, which in her view had wantonly squandered the southern insurgent movement."[17]

Military historian Shelby Stanton has written: "The Vietcong had performed most of the assaults and took such heavy losses that they were largely destroyed as an effective military menace to the South Vietnamese government."[18] Henry Kissinger wrote in one of his many works: "Militarily, Tet is now considered a major Communist defeat."[19] Col. Harry G. Summers Jr. sums it up this way:

> But it was not the United States that was defeated on the battlefield. It was the North Vietnamese Army and especially the Vietcong. Their "general offensive and general uprising" had been a tactical disaster. Not only had their military forces been resoundingly defeated, but their ideological illusion that the South Vietnamese people would flock to their banner during the "general uprising" proved false. From Tet 1968 on, the NVA realized it would not be able to attain its political objective with guerrilla forces and increasingly the war became an affair for the regular forces of the NVA.[20]

The previous quote concerning the nature of the war and its becoming ever increasingly a North Vietnamese affair reinforces information previously discussed in chapter 6 of this book. The following also alludes to the disaster brought on the

Vietcong by the Tet Offensive and reiterates a very sinister motive for the Tet Offensive by the North Vietnamese:

> Although not all members of the NLF knew it then, they had indeed been acting as proxies for Hanoi, and those who persisted in thinking otherwise were eliminated in the end as unreliable. In the view of General Fred C. Weyand, this might even have been one of the purposes of the Tet offensive of 1968: "Applying the test of *cui bono* (for whose benefit) it can be seen that the real losers of Tet-68 were the South Vietnamese Communists (the Vietcong or PRG) who surfaced, led the attacks, and were destroyed in the process . . . Just as the Russians eliminated their Polish competitors [with] the Warsaw uprising, the North Vietnamese eliminated their Southern competitors with Tet-68. They thereby insured that the eventual outcome of the war would be a South Vietnam dominated and controlled, not by *South* Vietnamese Communists, but by the *North* Vietnamese."[21]

Despite all the foregoing information and the fact that it was a military victory for the U.S. and allied side:

> Nevertheless, the Tet Offensive turned into a major psychological victory for Hanoi. One can reflect with some melancholy on the course of events had American leaders stepped up pressure on the North Vietnamese main-force units, which were now deprived of their guerrilla shield. Had America really gone for broke, it is probable that Johnson would have achieved the unconditional negotiations he was proposing, and maybe even an unconditional cease-fire.[22]

By now it should be clear to the reader that there was a great contradiction surrounding Tet. How did a military victory translate into a psychological defeat? This question will be examined.

One of the stock answers to the question as to how Tet

was transformed from military victory into psychological defeat is that it was caused, wittingly or unwittingly, by the media. Gen. William Westmoreland was critical of the coverage by the media during the war. "Westmoreland and his supporters also claimed that television, and to a lesser extent the print media, transformed the Communist failure in the Tet Offensive into a 'psychological victory' for the North Vietnamese."[23] In probably the most extensive work concerning media coverage of Vietnam, "Peter Braestrup made the same charge in his book *Big Story,* noting that 'crisis journalism' had seldom 'veered so widely from reality' as in the coverage of the Tet Offensive."[24]

Very strong antimedia opinions have been uttered by some. G. Gordon Liddy has said, "The press, for example, reported the Tet Offensive by the North as a great enemy victory. It was not." "The American press helped the Communists do in the Vietnam War what the Nazi 'Fifth Column' could not do in World War II—destroy the morale and fighting spirit of the American home front."[25]

Walter Cronkite of CBS News was arguably the most reliable media personality in the United States. Prior to the Tet Offensive his reporting on the Vietnam War had been balanced and some say even bland. After he returned from Vietnam, where he had ventured to report on Tet, he delivered a new verdict on the war that shocked and depressed even President Johnson and probably heavily impacted on mainstream America. It occurred on February 27, 1968, as Cronkite said, "It seems more certain than ever that the bloody experience of Vietnam is to end in stalemate. . . . To say that we are closer to victory today is to believe, in the face of the evidence, the optimists who have been wrong in the past. To suggest that we are on the edge of defeat is to yield to unreasonable pessimism. To say we are mired in stalemate seems the only realistic, yet unsatisfactory, conclusion."[26]

The U.S. public was not happy with the idea of stalemate.

They believed or were convinced by the media that they had been told that the war had been progressing better than to have the war at a stalemate.

Probably the most effective communist attack during Tet was a very small operation and a total tactical failure. The Vietcong attempted to occupy the U.S. embassy. About twenty Vietcong blew a hole in the wall surrounding the embassy and entered the compound grounds. None of them ever occupied the embassy, and all of them were killed. Many Americans, however believed that the communists had seized control of the embassy. This belief was due to erroneous news coverage. Chet Huntley reported on NBC's evening news in prime time that "twenty suicide commandos are reported to be holding the first floor of the embassy."[27] "A half-hour later the same reports were 'confirmed' by UPI."[28]

There is no question that the scenes and the reporting concerning the embassy made an indelible impression on the mind of many Americans. "Many Americans never knew that these 'confirmed' reports had been totally in error."[29]

It is doubtful that anybody in the media was concerned about the false impressions that were being made on the public, either! In the fall of 1968 a group of junior producers suspected that NBC may have gotten it wrong about Tet. They approached senior producer Robert Northshield with an idea to do a series on Tet to set the record straight. Northshield's response to the idea as related by Reed Irvine: "Tet has been established in the public mind as a defeat therefore it was an American defeat."[30]

Peter Braestrup has said concerning the embassy incident, "Hanoi didn't claim a victory—psychological, symbolic or otherwise—at the embassy but American newsmen were quick to award Hanoi a major psychological triumph there."[31]

News reports seemed to confirm to many Americans that our forces in Vietnam were in dire straits. Frank McGee went way beyond Cronkite's stalemate scenario in a March 10, 1968, NBC News special when he reported, "The enemy now has the initiative; he has dramatically enlarged the area of combat; he has newer, more sophisticated weapons . . . the war as the Administration has defined it is being lost."[32] The reader should contrast this assessment to what is now known and accepted to be the status of the enemy after Tet.

Gloomy media depictions of the war were not limited to the Saigon area but also occurred at the northern marine base at Khe Sanh during Tet. The media attempted to portray Khe Sanh as another Dien Bien Phu (where the French were defeated and driven out of Vietnam). Bob Young of ABC and Walter Cronkite of CBS linked the victorious general of Dien Bien Phu, Vo Nguyen Giap, to the siege at Khe Sanh, and *Time Magazine* put him on their cover.[33] It was as if Giap's presence would cause the defeat of the marines at Khe Sanh to be a foregone conclusion.

Four C-130 transport planes had been shot down attempting to resupply during the siege, and this gave television reporters what they desired the most, an eye-catching photo opportunity for the eyes of television viewers. The flaming planes were a sight seen by millions in their living rooms. Reporters were also delighted when enemy rockets exploded the ammo dump at Khe Sanh, as this was another great photo opportunity.

Newsweek magazine jumped on the antiwar bandwagon with its March 18, 1968, issue. It used the Khe Sanh ammo dump explosion as its cover, failing to let its readers know that the incident had occurred two months earlier, and then concluded: "Though the U.S dilemma at Khe Sanh is particularly acute, it is not unique. It simply reflects in microcosm the entire U.S. military position in Vietnam. U.S. strategy up to this point has been a failure."[34]

It is too bad that Newsweek didn't convince the United

States that what was **really** going on at Khe Sanh, as opposed to the way the media portrayed it, was the microcosm of the U.S. effort in the war. William Jayne, a Marine veteran at Khe Sanh, said, "The North Vietnamese never mounted a determined ground offensive against us."[35] The media never reported that unlike the French at Dien Bien Phu, U.S. Marines controlled the high ground around Khe Sanh. The siege at Khe Sanh lasted from January 21, 1968, until April 15, 1968. Americans killed in action totalled 199, and wounded amounted to 1600. In contrast, the North Vietnamese are estimated to have had an estimated 14,000 killed at Khe Sanh. Khe Sanh probably **was** a microcosm of U.S. military success during the war.

Those in the media who did realize that the Tet Offensive was a military debacle for the communists switched to the line of what masterful strategy the offensive was anyway, because despite it being a military loss it was a great psychological victory. Tran Do, who was one of the communist generals in charge of the Tet attacks, denied that there was a political objective. He said that the political impact "was an accidental byproduct."[36] That accidental byproduct some think was caused by the U.S. media.

Enough information has been given to the reader to make some judgments concerning the role of the media during Tet. Were they just reporting the facts, or were they unwitting aids to the enemy due to their adversarial relationship to the U.S. military? A bigger question would be whether Tet changed the media's mind about the war and caused them to undermine the military effort for the remainder of the war.

Others agree that the media played a role in turning the Tet military victory into a defeat but add that there was another factor that contributed to this phenomenon. Col. Harry G. Summers Jr. has written "that the real answer has to do with the collapse of the nation's 'national command authority,' the top level chain of command, including the president, the secretary of defense and the Joint Chiefs of Staff (JCS)."[37]

The Tet Offensive is said to have caused the psychological defeat of President Johnson concerning the Vietnam War. The question is why? During U.S. history there have been worse military setbacks than Tet. The Battle of the Bulge in World War II and the Chinese intervention in Korea are just a couple of examples. President Roosevelt (Battle of the Bulge) and President Truman (Chinese intervention in Korea) survived these setbacks and were able to effectively rally themselves and the country.

Colonel Summers has speculated that there were two reasons for Lyndon Johnson's reaction to Tet: "One reason is that Johnson's heart was not in the war to begin with. He saw both the war and the military itself as threats to his Great Society programs."[38] Given his relatively unenthusiastic support of the war to begin with, Tet made it easy to psychologically give up.

The second reason has emerged more recently. Summers has written:

> But in recent years, a more disturbing reason has emerged. Where Roosevelt and Truman could count on the steadfastness of their national security advisers, Johnson was let down by those he trusted.
>
> Eleven years after Johnson's death and 16 years after the Tet Offensive, Defense Secretary Robert McNamara, LBJ's principal military advisor, confessed that as early as 1965 or 1966, even as the American buildup in Vietnam began, he believed the war "could not be won militarily."[39]

Given McNamara's beliefs concerning the war, it is no surprise that he could not or would not rally the president and the country after Tet. McNamara, in fact, resigned as secretary of defense a month after the Tet Offensive.

McNamara's successor, Clark Clifford, was not an improvement on this score: "Twenty-three years after he was brought in to support Johnson's policies, Clifford brags in his 1991 memoir, *Counsel to the President,* that from the first he set out to 'impress upon the President that our posture is basically so impossible that we have to find some way out.'"[40] Clifford not only attempted to convince President Johnson of a way out but also undermined Johnson's policies. Historian Lewis Sorley notes: "It is one thing to seek to influence the formulation of policy, quite another to faithlessly undermine that policy once formulated. Clifford represents himself as being very proud of doing the latter."[41]

The Joint Chiefs of Staff (JCS) eliminated all chance of rallying President Johnson and the country by its actions. The JCS believed that the U.S. military was overextended because of the Vietnam War. This belief was bolstered by the North Korean seizure of the USS *Pueblo* in 1968 and what appeared to be a developing crisis in Berlin. The JCS solution to the problem was to mobilize the reserves.

> The Joint Chiefs could have made a straight-forward request for additional manpower to meet these strategic requirements. They also could have told Johnson that Vietnam was not as bad as it seemed.
>
> Instead, they chose to argue for more troops by portraying the war in Vietnam as much worse than it really was. They used Tet as a pretext to force Johnson to mobilize the reserves.
>
> And they double-dealed Gen. William Westmoreland, the U.S. commander in the field, as well.
>
> In a visit to Saigon, JCS Chairman Gen. Earle G. Wheeler convinced Westmoreland to request an additional 206,000 troops, which could be used to take the offensive in Vietnam. When he briefed Johnson, however, Wheeler made no mention of this new strategy. Rather, he painted a gloomy picture of the situation in Vietnam.[42]

Wheeler got Westmoreland, who thought the extra troops would be used to finish off a deeply wounded enemy in Vietnam, to request the additional troops. Wheeler wanted the troops for other reasons and simultaneously painted a gloomy picture of Vietnam to President Johnson, thereby reinforcing Johnson's defeatist attitude.

Needless to say, somebody leaked the troop request to the press. The press then relayed it to the U.S. public. When the public heard about it they assumed the additional troops were necessary, contrary to what General Westmoreland felt, because the situation in Vietnam was terrible after Tet. The request for the additional troops convinced the U.S. people that they had been lied to concerning the results of the Tet Offensive. This contributed to turning public opinion increasingly against the war. Robert McNamara, Clark Clifford, and Gen. Earl Wheeler all engaged in duplicity that greatly undermined Johnson and the war effort in Vietnam after the Tet Offensive. The national chain of command appears to have collapsed after Tet.

In addition to the feelings of betrayal, valid or not, the public felt concerning the official portrayal of results of Tet, many felt they had been deceived about the progress of the war also. The argument was advanced that General Westmoreland and the military in general had been painting too rosy of a picture of U.S. success up to the fall of 1967. Detractors argued that if the U.S. effort had been going so well, the enemy would not have been able to mount an offensive as massive as Tet.

Gen. William Westmoreland has a counter to that type of reasoning and argument. He explained what he thought the enemy's status and position were just prior to Tet:

Only desperate times could provoke such desperate measures, and the truth is that the enemy was hurting. They were winning no victories on the battlefield, and the time had come for them to reassess their strategy, to make a "momentous decision." The enemy had four choices. He could quit, but that was hardly in keeping with Communist ideology or methods. He could return to purely guerrilla warfare, but combined American, South Vietnamese, and allied strength would assure that he could accomplish little by that. He could go on the way he was going, which was to hope that the Americans, like the French before them would eventually become disenchanted. But if the decision was to be "momentous" it would have to be all out. Thus the North Vietnamese decided to "go for broke."[43]

Many in the United States felt that Tet proved that they had been lied to and deceived. "Few recalled that a force on the downgrade often tries to recover by means of some spectacular surge, as Adolf Hitler did with his surprise attack in the Ardennes in 1944 during the Battle of the Bulge."[44] Thus it may have been with Tet.

The feeling of betrayal as reflected in dwindling support of the war after Tet is reflected in opinion polls. A Gallup Poll taken in late February 1968 can be compared to a similar one taken three months earlier: "Just your impression, do you think that the U.S. and its allies are losing ground in Vietnam, standing still, or making progress?"

	November 1967	February 1968
Losing	8%	23%
Standing still	33%	38%
Making progress	50%	33%
No opinion	9%	6%[45]

The following statement reinforces the post-Tet losing of approval of the war. "But approval of Johnson's conduct of it, which had risen to 40 percent as a result of the 1967 public relations campaign, plummeted to an all-time low of 26 percent during Tet. By March moreover, an overwhelming majority of Americans (78 percent) were certain that the United States was not making any progress in Vietnam."[46] The Tet Offensive had taken its toll on U.S. public opinion, whatever the reason.

Next it will be analyzed how the Tet Offensive is being portrayed today. An examination of the high school textbooks will follow. This examination should give the reader a chance to determine how accurately the portrayal of this pivotal event is being depicted for the future.

These United States, the Questions of Our Past has this to say about the Tet Offensive:

> The greatest blow to hawk confidence came in early 1968 when, during the Vietnamese Lunar New Year (Tet), the Vietcong and North Vietnamese launched a major offensive against Saigon and other South Vietnamese cities. After fierce and bloody fighting, the attack was checked and the attackers forced to pay a high price, but Tet made a mockery of the administration's confident propaganda. Until this point many Americans had found it possible to believe that the war, however protracted, was being won. Tet seemed to show that the enemy was, if anything, growing in strength.[47]

There are some weaknesses in this textbook's narrative concerning the Tet Offensive. It is very inflammatory to depict the U.S. administration's assessment of the progress of the war as "confident propaganda." General Westmoreland's view of the situation in the fall of 1967 is that the enemy was on the ropes and that the Tet Offensive was a desperate attempt for a great victory. This hardly constitutes propaganda.

Tet also did not show that the "enemy was, if anything, growing in strength," as the textbook narrative indicated. To the contrary, previous information discussed in the present chapter of this work has established that the enemy, particularly the Vietcong, was reeling and had been weakened severely by the Tet Offensive.

Also absent from textbook narrative is any mention of the

139

fact that the enemy's expected general uprising did not occur. Given that this was a major objective of the offensive, it would seem relevant to mention that it did not occur.

The next textbook examined is *American Voices, a History of the United States 1865 to Present*. It does give an accurate report of what happened, and it does indicate that Tet was a military victory for the United States. This text also accurately states: "Even when it became clear that U.S. troops had the upper hand, much of the public refused to believe that Tet was anything but a setback."[48] It is interesting that this text pointed out this discrepancy but offered no explanation or elaboration as to why it existed.

This text also failed to point out that the enemy's general uprising did not occur. It also failed to recognize how extensively the enemy had been hurt by the Tet Offensive.

Todd & Curti's The American Nation states: "North Vietnam expected the Tet Offensive to bring down the government in the South as people rallied behind their 'liberators.' But Hanoi was disappointed. When the assault was over, more than a month later, an estimated 40,000 Communist soldiers lay dead."[49] Once again, in this textbook there is no emphasis on the failure to have a general uprising of the South Vietnamese.

The same text states: "But despite suffering heavy losses, the NLF remained strong in many places. They had faced overwhelming U.S. firepower and were still standing—more determined than ever to fight on."[50]

It is debatable that the NLF remained strong in many places and was more determined than ever to fight on. It is a known fact that the NLF was decimated by Tet and that the North Vietnamese had to fill the vacuum with more and more North Vietnamese troops.

Balanced presentation would have included an assessment of the Army of the Republic of Vietnam (ARVN) status after Tet. It would have been found that this much-maligned ally of the United States fought valiantly and maintained discipline throughout Tet. Many had expected the ARVN to fall apart in the face of military action such as occurred during the Tet Offensive. It did not!

This text also states that "the Tet offensive dealt a double blow: it indicated that U.S. leaders had misled the public, and it exposed severe flaws in U.S. military operations in Vietnam."[51]

Once again the idea of U.S. leadership misleading the public has been portrayed as fact. While it is a fact that the U.S. public had perceived that they had been misled, it is not a fact that they were.

If, in fact, Tet exposed severe flaws in U.S. military operations, it would be interesting to the informed person to know what these flaws were. Forty thousand enemy killed versus two thousand Americans killed during the Tet battles does not support the idea that the U.S. military had flaws. Since the battles were won by the U.S. forces, what, then, were the flaws in U.S. military operations?

An earlier version of Todd and Curti's *Triumph of the American Nation* contains this passage concerning the Tet Offensive: "Also, the Viet Cong gained firm control of large areas of the countryside."[52] The idea that the Vietcong gained control of large areas of the countryside as a result of the Tet Offensive is simply in error.

The textbook *The National Experience, a History of the United States* included this passage about Tet: "In February 1968, during the Tet holiday, the lunar New Year, a massive enemy offensive took American and South Vietnamese forces by surprise, convulsed 30 provincial capitals, and even penetrated the American embassy in Saigon. While the North Vietnamese failed to achieve their objectives and suffered grievous loses, the Tet offensive destroyed what remained of the Johnson administrations's credibility on Vietnam."[53]

A previously discussed misconception, the penetration of

the U.S. embassy, is repeated in this passage. Enemy soldiers did not get into the U.S. embassy, as had been erroneously reported by the media during the offensive. Most likely, readers of the previous passage would conclude that the enemy did get into the embassy.

The passage does state the North Vietnamese did not achieve their objectives. It does not emphasize that the general uprising did not occur. It also does not discuss how and why the administration's credibility was destroyed. Did the administration have no credibility or was it portrayed that way and perceived that way by the American public?

National Experience, to its credit, does portray a different point of view by including excerpts from *A Soldier Reports,* by Gen. William C. Westmoreland. This passage is included: "Yet even with the handicap of a graduated response, the war could have still been brought to a favorable end following defeat of the enemy's Tet offensive in 1968."[54] The problem is that the textbook narrative itself does not integrate this into its main body and give it credibility equal to the other statements in the book.

These samples of high school textbooks repeat many of the misconceptions that originally came from erroneous media reporting during the war. The textbooks have not examined, to any degree, new or conflicting scholarship concerning the Tet Offensive. Historical perceptions of the Tet Offensive that are unbalanced in nature are being perpetuated for future generations.

It is hoped that this book has exposed the reader to some differing interpretations of the Tet Offensive. It is agreed that this event was the most pivotal event of the Vietnam War, and therefore it is extremely important to have a wide range of interpretations of the actions and occurrences of this event.

I hope some understanding has been gained into the phenomenon of the military victory of Tet being transformed into a defeat in the eyes of the U.S. people. More important, how and why this phenomena occurred has been made understandable.

Notes

1. Harry G. Summers, "Turning Point of the War," *Vietnam Magazine,* February 1993, p. 23.
2. Bernard Brodie, "The Tet Offensive," in Noble Frankland and Christopher Dowling, eds., *Decisive Battles of the Twentieth Century* (London: Sidwick and Jackson, 1976), p. 321.
3. Robert F. Turner, *Vietnamese Communism, Its Origins and Development* (Stanford, CA: Hoover Institution Publications, 1975), p. 249.
4. Ibid.
5. Shelby Stanton, "The 273rd Viet Cong Regiment Was Bloodied While Trying to Take Saigon, but It Survived to Fight Again," *Vietnam Magazine,* February 1993.
6. Ibid.
7. William C. Westmoreland, "What Did the North Vietnamese Hope to Gain with Their 1968 Tet Offensive? Were They after the Cities, or More?" *Vietnam Magazine,* February 1993, p. 64.
8. Ibid., p. 65.
9. Ibid., p. 68.
10. Neil Sheehan, et al., eds., *The Pentagon Papers* (New York: Quadrangle, 1971), p. 617.
11. Nguyen Van Canh, *Vietnam under Communism* (Stanford, CA: Hoover Institution Press, 1983), p. 10.
12. Ibid.
13. Fox Butterfield, "The New Vietnam Scholarship," *New York Times Magazine,* February 13, 1983, p. 56.
14. Ibid.
15. Robert F. Turner, *Vietnamese Communism, Its Origins and Development* (Stanford, CA: Hoover Institution Publications, 1975), p. 252.
16. Stanley Karnow, *Vietnam, a History, the First Complete Account of Vietnam at War* (New York: Penguin, 1983), p. 204.
17. Ibid., p. 545.
18. Shelby Stanton, *The Rise and Fall of an American Army* (Novato, CA: Presidio, 1985), p. 245.
19. Henry Kissinger, *Diplomacy* (New York: Simon and Schuster, 1994), p. 670, citing Guenter Lewy, *America in Vietnam* (New York: Oxford Uni-

versity Press, 1978), p. 76, and Don Oberdorfer, *Tet* (Garden City, NY: Doubleday, 1971), p. 329.

20. Harry G. Summers Jr., *Vietnam War Almanac* (New York: Facts on File, 1985), p. 335.

21. Harry G. Summers Jr., *On Strategy* (Carlisle Barracks, PA: U.S. Army War College Strategic Studies Institute, 1981), p. 61.

22. Kissinger, *Diplomacy*, pp. 670–71.

23. Randy Roberts, *Television's Vietnam, a Visual Investigation* (CD-ROM) (Redmond, WA: Medio Multimedia, 1994.)

24. Peter Braestrup, *Big Story: How the American Press and Television Reported and Interpreted the Crisis of Tet 1968 in Vietnam and Washington,* (Boulder, CO: Westview, 1977), quoted in Roberts, *Television*.

25. Bill McCloud, *What Should We Tell Our Children about Vietnam?* (Norman: University of Oklahoma Press, 1989), p. 74.

26. Videotape, *The Vietnam War With Walter Cronkite, the Tet Offensive* (New York: CBS News, 1985).

27. Don Oberdorfer, *Tet!* (Garden City, NY: Doubleday, 1971), p. 28.

28. Ibid., p. 31.

29. Turner, *Vietnamese Communism*, p. 253.

30. Videotape, *Television's Vietnam Part Two: The Impact of Media* (Washington, DC: Accuracy in Media, 1984, 1985).

31. Ibid.

32. Ronald H. Spector, *After Tet the Bloodiest Year in Vietnam* (New York: Free Press, 1993), p. 5.

33. *Television's Vietnam*.

34. Ibid.

35. Ibid.

36. Butterfield, "The New Vietnam Scholarship," p. 56.

37. Summers, "Turning Point of the War," p. 23.

38. Harry G. Summers Jr., "In Washington: Defeat Snatched from Victory," *American Legion Magazine,* February 1993, p. 52.

39. Ibid.

40. Ibid.

41. Ibid.

42. Ibid.

43. Westmoreland, "What Did the North Vietnamese Hope?," p. 62.

44. Ibid., p. 70.

45. Turner, *Vietnamese Communism*, p. 254.

46. Louis Harris, *The Anguish of Change* (New York: 1973,) pp. 63–64, and Bruce W. Roper, "What Public Opinion Polls Said," in Braestrup, *Big Story*, pp. 677–704.

47. Irwin Unger, *These United States, the Questions of Our Past* (Englewood Cliffs, NJ: Prentice Hall, 1995), p. 845.

48. Carol Berkin et al., *American Voices, a History of the United States, 1865 to Present* (Glenview, IL: Scott Foresman, 1995), p. 740.
49. Paul Boyer, *Todd & Curti's The American Nation* (Austin, TX: Holt, Rhinehart, and Winston, 1995), p. 879.
50. Ibid.
51. Ibid., p. 880.
52. Lewis Paul Todd and Merle Curti, *Triumph of the American Nation* (Orlando, FL: Harcourt, Brace, and Jovanovich, 1986), p. 922.
53. John M. Blum, ed., *The National Experience, a History of the United States* (Fort Worth, TX: Harcourt, Brace, and Jovanovich, 1993), p. 861.
54. Ibid., p. 860.

8

Into Cambodia

On April 7, 1970, Pres. Richard Nixon made a televised address to the nation. In this address he announced that U.S. troops were moving into the country of Cambodia. To many people this announcement seemingly widened the Vietnam War into the U.S. version of the Indochina War. To President Nixon and others the move into Cambodia was not a widening of the war but a temporary incursion to expedite Nixon's Vietnamization program. Vietnamization, as the reader will recall, was the gradual withdrawal of U.S. troops as the South Vietnamese became capable of taking on more and more of the burden of fighting.

This chapter will examine whether the movement into Cambodia was an invasion or an incursion. Those who believe that it was an invasion also felt that the Cambodian move was a widening or expansion of the war into yet another Southeast Asian country and that this was contrary to the wishes of the American people, who wanted a conclusion to a drawn-out war. "When this operation was announced, the critics charged that it would increase American casualties, that it would widen the war, that it might postpone troop withdrawals."[1]

Those who were on the other side viewed the move into Cambodia as an incursion that was of temporary nature. It was not an expansion of the war but, in fact, a way to end the war more rapidly.

It is the contention of this book that the invasion thesis

was given more credibility by the media and academia of that time and has been the position of mainstream history also. The evidence of the incursion thesis will be examined thoroughly in this chapter as an alternative explanation of the move into Cambodia.

There is no doubt that the movement of U.S. troops into Cambodia in late April 1970 created a furor in this country.

The day after President Nixon's televised announcement of the invasion on April 30, public protests disrupted colleges throughout the country. In Schenectady, New York, Union College students burned Richard Nixon in effigy, then blocked downtown traffic. One thousand University of Cincinnati students marched downtown and staged a ninety-minute demonstration. Similar outbursts occurred at colleges in Georgia, Wisconsin, Texas, California, and almost every other state, At President Nixon's alma mater, Whittier College, at least a third of the student body denounced him. Before May was over, 57 percent of the country's 1,350 campuses experienced strikes against classes and protests involving 4.5 million students.[2]

Surely there was a massive amount of objection to the move into Cambodia on college campuses. The worst event during the protests, of course, was the killing of four students by Ohio National Guardsmen during antiwar protests at Kent State University on May 4, 1970.

A question to be asked is whether negative student reaction to the move into Cambodia was justified. To determine the answer to this question it is necessary to analyze the government's decision to send U.S. troops into Cambodia. What circumstances in Cambodia and its relationship to the Vietnam War prompted this action?

Cambodia was ruled by Prince Norodom Sihanouk. After the French withdrawal from Indochina in 1954 Sihanouk tried to preserve Cambodia's neutrality. By 1965, however, both the

147

Vietcong and the North Vietnamese had established large base areas in eastern Cambodia. From these base camps they conducted military operations against U.S. and South Vietnamese forces in South Vietnam. They would cross the border, go on the offensive, and then retreat when necessary to the safety of the Cambodian sanctuaries. There they had a safe haven from U.S. and South Vietnamese forces.

It is interesting to note that the North Vietnamese and the Vietcong had been violating Cambodian neutrality since 1965. In 1970 when the United States moved into Cambodia a double standard emerged. Much world and U.S. antiwar opinion accused the United States of violating Cambodia's neutrality. The reader should note that there would have been no reason for the United States to move into Cambodia unless the North Vietnamese and Vietcong had been there first. Somehow this fact was lost on the antiwar factions of the United States and the world.

"With the tacit approval of Prince Sihanouk, President Nixon ordered the so-called 'secret' bombing of these Cambodian base areas to take pressure off the ongoing U.S. troop withdrawal from Vietnam and to put pressure on the North Vietnamese to enter into serious negotiations."[3] Nixon had already reduced U.S. troop strength in Vietnam by 65,000 and in 1970 announced he planned to reduce it by another 150,000 during that year.

Make no mistake whom Cambodia's Prince Sihanouk viewed as the threat to his neutrality and independence during the time prior to 1970.

Sihanouk's public statements of the period leave no doubt as to whom he considered the threat to his country's independence. Repeatedly and publicly he protested North Vietnamese "aggression" and infringement of Cambodia's sovereignty. In June 1969—three months after the secret bombing

148

started—he had complained at a press conference that Cambodia's Ratanakiri province was "practically North Vietnamese territory," and that "Viet Minh" (North Vietnamese) and Vietcong had heavily infiltrated into Svay Rieng province.[4]

By the middle of March 1970 the situation in Cambodia was beginning to change drastically. Unrest in Cambodia led to the deposing of Prince Sihanouk while he was visiting Moscow. He was replaced by Gen. Lon Nol, who was friendly with U.S. interests.

Prince Sihanouk's reaction to his overthrow was to violently turn against the United States and throw in his lot with the North Vietnamese. Sihanouk, in effect, declared it his intention to struggle to overthrow those who had overthrown him. He declared war against his former government in Pnom Penh.

Henry Kissinger relates: "In short, by the middle of April, *before* we had taken *any* significant action, Sihanouk had irrevocably joined forces with the Communists, the Communists had dedicated themselves to the overthrow of the Pnom Penh government, and North Vietnamese units were attacking deep inside Cambodia."[5] Cambodia's premier, Lon Nol, said, "There is no need to declare war. It is already a *fait accompli.* This is war."[6]

President Nixon and the United States were at a crossroads. The North Vietnamese were pledged to helping Sihanouk restore his power in Cambodia. If they were successful, Cambodia would be a puppet government of the North Vietnamese. It also would be an open-ended staging area from which to mount attacks on South Vietnam that would jeopardize Vietnamization, U.S. troop safety, and U.S. troop withdrawal. A North Vietnamized Cambodia would deeply jeopardize the U.S. effort in Vietnam.

Given the situation, President Nixon made his decision to

move into Cambodia. He announced the movement on a nationwide television address and spelled out very clearly what our objectives were and how we were to attain those objectives in Cambodia and Vietnam.

In his speech, President Nixon enunciated concern for the U.S. troops in Vietnam. He said:

> After full consultation with the *National Security Council, Ambassador Bunker,* General *Abrams,* and my other advisers, I have concluded that the actions of the enemy in the last ten days clearly endanger the lives of Americans who are in Vietnam now and would constitute an unacceptable risk to those who will be there after *withdrawal* of another 150,000.
>
> To protect our men who are in Vietnam and to guarantee the continued success of our withdrawal and *Vietnamization* programs, I have concluded that the time has come for action. (Emphasis added)[7]

Nixon explained that the United States would join with the South Vietnamese to clean out enemy sanctuaries in Cambodia:

> Our third choice is to go to the heart of the trouble. That means cleaning out major North Vietnamese and *Vietcong*-occupied territories—these sanctuaries which serve as bases for attacks on both Cambodia and American and South Vietnamese forces in South Vietnam. Some of these, incidentally, are as close to *Saigon* as Baltimore is to Washington. This one, for example [indicating], is called the *Parrot's Beak.* It is only thirty-three miles from Saigon. (Emphasis added)[8]

While announcing that U.S. forces would move into Cambodia that night, Nixon also addressed the issue of Cambodian neutrality: "This key control center has been occupied by the

North Vietnamese and Vietcong for five years in blatant violation of Cambodia's neutrality."[9]

Nixon emphasized that this was not an invasion of Cambodia and that the movement of troops was temporary: "This is not an invasion of Cambodia. The areas in which these attacks will be launched are completely occupied and controlled by North Vietnamese forces. Our purpose is not to occupy the areas. Once enemy forces are driven out of these sanctuaries and once their military supplies are destroyed, we will withdraw."[10] Nixon made it very clear what the movement into Cambodia was about.

Despite the clearly defined nature of the incursion, U.S. college students, many of their professors, and politicians in Washington, D.C., decided to view the incursion as a widening of the war. The media for the most part portrayed it the same way. It is interesting that such a learned and informed group did not care to understand what President Nixon was doing.

Even after the operation was over and it turned out that Nixon did just what he had pledged to do, these groups did not see it the way Nixon did. As mentioned earlier, critics said that it would widen the war, increase casualties, and postpone troop withdrawals. As the president reported after the incursion, "But the operation was undertaken for the opposite reasons—and it has had precisely the opposite effect."[11]

Nixon went on to summarize the successes of the incursion into Cambodia. He said that we had eliminated the threat to the security of the remaining Americans in Vietnam and bought some time for the South Vietnamese to further prepare themselves for their own defense. We also had ensured the continuation and success of our troop withdrawal. Fifty thousand of the previously promised 150,000 troops to be withdrawn were to be withdrawn by October 15, 1970.[12]

The Cambodian incursion was credited with being successful by other sources also. Gen. Donn A. Starry was a colo-

151

nel at the time of the Cambodian incursion. He was the commander of the Eleventh Armored Cavalry Regiment, which was one of the leading U.S. ground forces that moved into Cambodia. Starry relates his view of U.S. success in Cambodia:

> By the end of June free world forces in Cambodia had captured or destroyed almost ten thousand tons of matériel and food. In terms of enemy needs this amount was enough rice to feed more than 25,000 troops a full ration for an entire year; individual weapons to equip 55 full-strength battalions; and mortar, rocket, and recoilless rifle ammunition for more than 9,000 average attacks against free world units. In all, 11,362 enemy soldiers were killed and over 2,000 captured.
>
> These statistics are impressive, and without a doubt the Cambodian expeditions had crippled the Viet Cong and North Vietnamese operations, but the most important results cannot be measured in tangibles alone. The armor-led attacks into Cambodia by units from Military Region 4 had been well planned, well coordinated, and well carried out. They were generally conducted without the massive U.S. ground support typical of operations from Military Region 3, yet they severely hurt the enemy. The South Vietnamese, their morale high, returned to resume pacification of the delta, a goal which had suddenly come much closer to realization.[13]

Vietnamization was both tested and hastened by the Cambodian incursion. Troung Nhu Tang, the minister of justice of the NLF, said, "The American bombing and invasion of Cambodia largely accomplished its immediate goals (I barely survived it myself). Nixon and Kissinger justified it then and later as an operation that gained an essential year of time."[14]

Shelby Stanton described the seizure of enemy supplies: "The sizes of the depots being uncovered were beyond belief. One depot complex contained so many military stores that it was promptly dubbed the City. The large storage areas were packed with new supplies and cargo trucks, neatly arranged and obviously abandoned in a hurry."[15] It is clear that this constituted a massive setback for America's enemy.

"Militarily, the operation in Cambodia was a huge success. At the time, however, we were mercilessly attacked at home for our efforts to help South Vietnam and Cambodia survive."[16] This merciless attack that President Nixon referred to may have been a less than accurate perception as to how Americans in general viewed the incursion into Cambodia.

Dramatic and widespread as the antiwar violence and turmoil were, a sizeable portion of Americans voiced both their support for the President's decision to invade Cambodia and their anger toward antiwar protestors. A *Newsweek* poll in the second week of May showed 50 percent approval of President Nixon's decision. Those polled also deplored the protesters' tumultuous behavior. Fifty-eight percent blamed students for what happened at Kent State.[17]

An event right after the incursion is probably one of the best-kept secrets of journalism and history. Rarely is this event recorded in written history concerning the Cambodian incursion. "On May 20, 100,000 construction workers, stevedores, tradesmen, and office clerks marched through Manhattan to City Hall in a display of support for President Nixon."[18] Rarely, if ever, does any video coverage of this event appear in the various video productions that purport to be histories of the Vietnam War.

"A large proportion of the American people, traditionally loyal to the president in crucial moments, supported the Cambodian incursion."[19] This may have been true with mainstream America, but as Stanley Karnow put it: "Once again, however, the opinion leaders set the pace. Press commentators lashed out at Nixon, with *The New York Times* calling the action a 'virtual renunciation' of his pledge to end the war and the *Wall Street Journal* warning against 'deeper entrapment' in Southeast Asia. Educators, clergyman, lawyers, businessmen and other protested."[20]

It is widely believed that educators played a large role in leading student protest against the Cambodian incursion as well as the war in Vietnam in general. University of California professor of sociology Robert Nisbet wrote in the British magazine *Encounter:* "Without faculty stimulus, financial contributions and other forms of assistance, the student revolt could never really have got off the ground."[21]

While a large amount of protest did occur concerning the Cambodian incursion, it is a mistake to think that this protest was the dominant mode of the country's feeling. "On balance, the President's decision to destroy Communist sanctuaries in Cambodia was given strong support."[22]

Examination of the high school textbooks shows that they leave something to be desired. If it is left to what is written in these textbooks American youth will receive an incomplete, imbalanced, and slanted view of the incursion into Cambodia.

None of the examined textbooks emphasized how successful the military operation was. There is no mention of the vast amounts of enemy equipment and matériel that were captured. Worst of all not one of the textbooks mentioned that the Cambodian incursion ensured that Vietnamization would progress more rapidly; therefore, U.S. troop withdrawals could be sped up and our role in the war ended more rapidly.

The North Vietnamese and Vietcong had occupied the neutral country of Cambodia for at least five years before the 1970 U.S. incursion. Some of the textbooks mention the enemy sanctuaries but do not emphasize the lengthy time period they had been used as a staging area to attack U.S. forces. None of them mention that after Lon Nol took power in Cam-

154

bodia he demanded that the North Vietnamese and Vietcong leave his country. Nor was it mentioned that instead the communists pledged themselves to conquering Cambodia and had begun military operations deep into it well before the U.S. incursion there, an incursion that the Lon Nol government approved.

American Voices, a History of the United States, 1865 to the Present refers to the sanctuaries: "In 1969 Nixon ordered American planes to destroy the supposed communist sanctuaries there."[23] It is a well-established fact that there were massive communist sanctuaries in Cambodia that had been there for a long period of time. Use of the word *supposed* in the text is an attempt to slant the readers' view and question as to whether the enemy was present in Cambodia.

Triumph of the American Nation refers to Americans who wanted a quick end to America's military involvement in Vietnam and says: "They were further disheartened in the spring of 1970 by Nixon's startling announcement that South Vietnamese and American troops were crossing the border into 'neutral' Cambodia."[24] At the time of the incursion, Cambodia was far from a neutral country. Lon Nol was happy to have U.S. and South Vietnamese forces fighting the Vietcong and North Vietnamese that he had asked to leave. Even prior to the Lon Nol takeover of the government, it is hard to classify Cambodia as neutral given the fact that Vietcong and North Vietnamese forces had been occupying the country since at least 1965.

These United States, the Questions of Our Past also cast doubt on the position that there were communist sanctuaries in Cambodia. Referring to President Nixon, they write: "American forces on a sweep through Cambodia to attack bases, which, he claimed were refuges for Vietcong guerrillas."[25] Use of "which he claimed" attempts to cast doubt on the validity of the attack on the base areas in Cambodia.

Todd & Curti's The American Nation also contains some

errors in its narrative. They write: "Publicly, Nixon emphasized Vietnamization; secretly, however, he planned to widen the war—into Cambodia."[26] Contrary to widening the war, the incursion into Cambodia was an attempt to reduce U.S. involvement in the war and there is no reason to believe that the Cambodian incursion and Vietnamization worked at cross purposes. This passage implies that the incursion would secretly work against Vietnamization.

By far the most damaging erroneous passage follows: "The invasion destroyed the delicate balance that had kept Cambodia out of the war. NVA troops were forced into the interior of Cambodia where battles with U.S. and ARVN forces destroyed much of the countryside."[27]

The incursion into Cambodia did not upset any delicate balance in Cambodia. A change of government had occurred in Cambodia prior to U.S. involvement. U.S. incursion did not force NVA forces into the interior; they had already sided with ousted Prince Norodom Sihanouk to overthrow the new government in Pnom Penh and were on the move militarily into the interior weeks before the U.S. incursion (see previous page). In fact, the reverse was true. Part of the reason that the United States moved into Cambodia was to prevent a North Vietnamese takeover of the country. The North Vietnamese had already moved some of their forces out of the sanctuary area near Vietnam's border to locations nearer interior Cambodia. The assertion that much of Cambodia's countryside was destroyed as U.S. and ARVN forces battled in the countryside cannot be substantiated, either.

It is very important to keep the matter of who destroyed any balance and neutrality in Cambodia straight. It was the North Vietnamese and Vietcong who violated Cambodia's neutrality in the first place. Second, it was the North Vietnamese making moves to conquer Cambodia after the Lon Nol takeover who prompted the United States to enter Cambodia.

Those who accuse the United States of upsetting the balance in Cambodia have a penchant for extrapolating that it was the fault of the United States when Pol Pot and his murderous Khmer Rouge caused the genocidal killing fields of Cambodia later. This train of thought needs to be nipped in the bud. The United States was not the foreign power that initially dragged Cambodia into the Indochina War; it was North Vietnam. Any genocidal results that occurred in the long run should be laid at the doorstep of the communists from North and South Vietnam who initiated the chain of events that led to these results.

Readers now should be able to better judge whether the U.S. incursion was an attempt to hasten Vietnamization and reduce our involvement in the war or an attempt to widen the war with an invasion of Cambodia. The incursion was an attack on foreigners to Cambodia using that country to fight a war in Vietnam. Military moves were against these invaders, and U.S. forces were withdrawn as promised after a limited time period. The incursion is said to have hastened Vietnamization by a year. Readers should judge for themselves whether America's move into Cambodia was an invasion or an incursion.

Notes

1. "The President Reports on the War in Cambodia," *U.S. News and World Report,* June 15, 1970, p. 78.
2. Samuel Lipsman and Edward Doyle, eds., *The Vietnam Experience, Fighting for Time* (Boston, MA: Boston Publishing, 1983), p. 178.
3. Harry G. Summers, Jr., *Vietnam War Almanac* (New York: Facts on File, 1985), p. 105.
4. Henry Kissinger, *White House Years* (Boston, MA: Little, Brown, 1979), p. 460.
5. Ibid., p. 468.
6. "Indochina's Crumbling Frontiers," *Time,* April 20, 1970, p. 24.
7. *Address by President Nixon on Cambodia, April 30, 1970,* U.S. Senate Committee on Foreign Relations, Background Information Relating to Southeast Asia and Vietnam (December 1974), pp. 345–47.

8. Ibid.
9. Ibid.
10. Ibid.
11. "The President Reports on the War in Cambodia," p. 78.
12. Ibid.
13. Donn A. Starry, *Armored Combat in Vietnam* (Salem, NH: Arno, 1980), p. 180.
14. Troung Nhu Tang, *A Vietcong Memoir, an Inside Account of the Vietnam War and Its Aftermath* (New York: Random House, 1985), p. 212.
15. Shelby Stanton, *The Rise and Fall of an American Army, U.S. Ground Forces in Vietnam, 1965–1973* (Novato, CA: Presidio, 1985), pp. 338–39.
16. Richard Nixon, *The Real War* (New York: Warner, 1980), p. 110.
17. Lipsman and Doyle, *The Vietnam Experience*, p. 182.
18. Ibid.
19. Stanley Karnow, *Vietnam, A History, the First Complete Account of Vietnam at War* (New York: Penguin, 1983), p. 610.
20. Ibid.
21. "Teachers Role in Campus Revolt," *U.S. News and World Report,* June 15, 1970, p. 37.
22. "Silent Majority Speaks Out on Nixon, Agnew, War, Students, a Survey," *U.S. News and World Report,* June 8, 1970, p. 34.
23. Carol Berkin et al., *American Voices, a History of the United States, 1865 to the Present* (Glenview, IL: Scott Foresman, 1995), p. 747.
24. Lewis Paul Todd and Merle Curti, *Triumph of the American Nation* (Orlando, FL: Harcourt, Brace, Jovanovich, 1986), p. 924.
25. Irwin Unger, *These United States, the Questions of Our Past* (Englewood Cliffs, NJ: Prentice Hall, 1995), p. 856.
26. Paul Boyer, *Todd & Curti's The American Nation* (Austin, TX: Holt, Rhinehart, and Winston, 1995), p. 882.
27. Ibid.

9

The "Horror" of Vietnam

The United States has fought many wars in many places throughout its history. War by nature is full of horror and inflicts terrible consequences on those who are involved in it. To many, the Vietnam War has been portrayed and perceived as singularly the most brutal of the wars in which the United States has participated. This chapter will challenge the idea that the Vietnam War was uniquely "horrendous" and offer some insight into why it was portrayed as such.

One explanation of the Vietnam War being portrayed in such a negative fashion rests on the assertion that the antiwar movement had and still has a vested interest in portraying the war in that fashion. Col. Harry Summers has put it this way:

> One of the greatest ironies of the Vietnam War is that those still suffering most from that conflict are the ones who never served there. While the overwhelming majority of Vietnam veterans have long since returned to civilian life and got on with their lives and careers, many of the draft dodgers and war evaders still struggle with their consciences. Torn by guilt, they try to explain their evasion by deliberately distorting what the war was all about. . . . One of the most pernicious myths is their contention that the war in Vietnam was uniquely horrendous—the most heinous, the most brutal, and the most inhumane war in the history of mankind.[1]

A. Francis Hatch frames the issue in this fashion: "How, in

America, had that image become so distorted? It was the result of a deliberate and vituperative campaign of propaganda and disinformation promulgated and perpetuated by leaders in the anti-war movement to advance their own political agendas. That campaign went unchallenged, indeed was supported, by the dominant media establishment in America."[2]

The war was portrayed that way then and it continues to be portrayed similarly up into the present. The vested interests that led to distortion of the events of the Vietnam War while it occurred have perpetuated that version of the history of the war up to present day.

This chapter will examine some of the distortions that led to the categorization of the war as uniquely horrendous. I hope the reader will be exposed to the misinformation that was and still is part of the Vietnam experience.

One of the events of the war that was the target of distortion was the so-called Christmas bombing of December 1972. This operation was called Linebacker II. American antiwar activists made the charge that it involved carpet bombing—i.e., the deliberate targeting of civilian areas with intensive bombing designed to "carpet" (completely cover) a city with bombs, as in Dresden during World War II—of Hanoi.[3] Col. Harry Summers further commented:

In 1974, on my first journey to Hanoi, I fully expected to see what I had seen in Yokohama in 1947, or in Berlin in 1953, cities that had been indeed carpet bombed. But as our negotiating team traveled from the airport and across the Paul Doumer bridge into the city itself, I was truly shocked at how thoroughly I had been deceived. Instead of a city flattened to the ground I saw a city which evidenced no sign of bomb damage whatsoever. Old French colonial housing, not rubble, stretched in all directions.

The city undoubtedly had been hit during the bombing attacks. But any fair minded observer could clearly see that it had never been carpet bombed.[4]

Stanley Karnow referring to Hanoi has written:

American antiwar activists visiting the city during the attacks urged the mayor to claim a death toll of ten thousand. He refused, saying that his government's credibility was at stake. The official North Vietnamese figure for civilian fatalities for the period was 1,318 in Hanoi and 305 in Haiphong—hardly the equivalent of the Americans' incendiary bombing of Tokyo in March 1945, for example, when nearly eighty-four thousand people were killed in a single night. The comparison is, of course, irrelevant, except that the Christmas bombings of Hanoi have been depicted as another Hiroshima.[5]

It is very interesting indeed that Americans in Hanoi were willing to vilify the U.S. effort in the war more than the North Vietnamese themselves. The U.S. antiwar activists wanted the fatalities to be reported as more than five times the actual figure! North Vietnamese officials, very adept at propaganda, would not even go that far.

U.S. high school textbooks perpetuate the notion presented by the antiwar element to this day. *The National Experience, a History of the United States* puts it this way: "Over Christmas, in one of the most savage acts of a savage war, Nixon ordered the bombing of Hanoi and Haiphong, with B-52's smashing the North Vietnamese cities for twelve days."[6]

Another textbook, *American Voices, a History of the United States, 1865 to the Present* records it this way: "The raids, known as the Christmas bombing, continued for 12 days. Hanoi and Haiphong were particularly hard hit, and many civilians were killed."[7]

Once it was discovered that, in fact, civilian casualties were low during the Christmas bombings, the antiwar faction's explanation advanced was that these casualties were low because the populations of Hanoi and Haiphong had largely been evacuated to the countryside. Stanley Karnow wrote: "But that thesis skirts the fact, as I observed in 1981, that most of the buildings in both cities were neither demolished nor reconstructed. In fact the B-52s were programmed to spare civilians, and they pinpointed their targets with extraordinary precision."[8]

U.S. bombing in Vietnam was always subject to hyperbole. Numerous written publications and videos have trumpeted the fact that a greater tonnage of U.S. bombs were dropped in the Vietnam War than in World War II. Walter Cronkite reports this in his 1985 video series on the Vietnam war. Cronkite says, "It staggers the imagination, the sheer volume of high explosives dropped in the Vietnam war. American warplanes delivered almost seven and a half million tons of bombs. More than three times our total for all of World War II. . . . Giant B-52s delivered a devastating payload. They left the earth below marked like a moonscape."[9]

What the reports of this massive bombing fail to emphasize is that the tonnage should not even be compared to World War II tonnage because, as Col. Harry G. Summers has written, "These tonnages are somewhat misleading, however, since most of the bombs were dropped on uninhabited jungle areas along the Ho Chi Minh trail in an unsuccessful attempt to block enemy infiltration."[10]

In the same Cronkite videotape is shown a report by Swedish reporter Eric Ericson that depicts nonmilitary targets including a North Vietnamese hospital hit during the Christmas bombing of 1972. Not shown in the original report but added briefly by Cronkite in the 1985 narration was the fact that the hospital was near an enemy airfield.

Original reporting of the war might allow a U.S. citizen to conclude that the United States was purposely bombing nonmilitary targets in Hanoi and other places. This conclusion, if it occurred, would have been a mistake, because the "North Vietnamese now freely admit that nonmilitary targets in the city itself were never specifically targeted."[11]

The United States, in fact, made pursuit of the war much more difficult for itself during much of the war due to concern for civilian casualties. When Robert McNamara was secretary of defense he initially drew a ten-mile circle around Hanoi and a five-mile circle around Haiphong (Hanoi's port city) within which no U.S. airpower was to be used.

> The North sensed McNamara's overconcern for collateral civilian casualties and responded in two ways. First they moved as much military equipment as they could into populated areas. In the case of anti-aircraft guns, some of the favorite sites were spots they knew were off-limits to our pilots, such as the center of villages, dikes that controlled flooding along the Red River delta, and the roofs of hospitals. Then they increased their propaganda about civilian casualties, and McNamara responded by adding a 30-mile restricted circle around the Hanoi prohibited circle and a 15-mile restricted circle around the Haiphong prohibited circle. Nobody was permitted inside the restricted circles without NcNamara's personal permission.[12]

As the reader should be able to surmise, it was not the United States that first purposely brought the tools of war into specific civilian areas. "The North knew where we could and could not go, so they moved most of their guns and SAMs into villages along routes we were forced to follow."[13] SAMs were surface-to-air missiles that were used to shoot down many of the planes that resulted in U.S. pilots becoming prisoners of war for extremely lengthy periods.

Despite knowledge of the previous things, the idea that the United States was pursuing a genocidal war was being perpetuated. It was accused of using indiscriminate firepower in free fire zones, resulting in unprecedented civilian casualties.

> One of the most misunderstood aspects of the Vietnam war, the very term "free fire zone," with its connotation of indiscriminate use of firepower, provoked an emotional reaction among many Americans. The irony was that in World War II, for example, the entire continent of Europe was generally a free fire zone, as was everything north of the front lines in the Korean war. In Vietnam an attempt was made to limit such indiscriminate use of firepower, and permission had to be received from Vietnamese province and district chiefs before artillery or air attacks could be made. Only uninhabited areas or areas totally under enemy control were approved by Vietnamese authorities as free fire zones.[14]

The concept of Vietnam's free fire zones being uniquely horrendous does not hold up under examination. It is obvious that these zones were less limited in other U.S. wars.

The idea that the United States was fighting a genocidal war is somewhat refuted by much of what has been said previously in this chapter. It is also refuted by a further examination of the facts. Genocide is murdering or attempting to murder an entire people. Citing the massive tonnage of bombs dropped in the Vietnam war generally went hand in hand to support the charge of genocide. When examined closely the facts do not give credibility to charges of genocide. "Yet at the very time charges of genocide were being made, it was known that the population of South Vietnam was *increasing*. Indeed, no less fervent an antiwar activist than Daniel Ellsberg, speaking in 1970, cautioned against use of the term 'genocide' by the movement 'even if it is strictly warranted,' because 'the population of South Vietnam has almost surely increased each year in the last five.'"[15]

So had the population of North Vietnam, despite charges that American bombing was taking a heavy toll of civilian casualties. According to the *United Nations Demographic Yearbook 1974*, the population of South Vietnam went from 16.12 million in 1965 to 19.95 million in 1973, and that of North Vietnam from 18.71 million in 1965 to 22.70 million in 1973; the annual rates of growth were roughly double that of the United States.[16]

The charge of indiscriminate firepower in Vietnam resulting in massive civilian casualties also needs to be placed in proper perspective.

Here, too, the charge can be characterized as "a bit grotesque." According to Lewy's calculations—which are generous in their definition of civilian and extremely cautious in their reliance on official "body counts"—the Vietnam War during the years of active American involvement was no more destructive of civilian life, both North and South, than other armed conflicts of this century and a good bit less than some, such as the Korean War. Whereas as many as 70 percent of those killed in Korea were civilians, in Vietnam the proportion was at most 45 percent, which was approximately the level of civilian casualties in World War II. And of course a substantial percentage of these civilians were killed not by the Americans or the South Vietnamese but by the Vietcong and North Vietnamese, especially after 1969, when there was a steady decline in American bombing and shelling and combat increasingly occurred farther away from areas in which the rural population lived.[17]

A different and telling perspective on the rules of engagement in the Vietnam War was manifested by the common complaint of the U.S. GI that far from being indiscriminate, American use of firepower was restricted too much and was too cautious. "The military fretted under the limitations, citing incidents in which they took casualties that might have been

165

avoided with more thorough preparatory bombing."[18] Limitations included were very burdensome clearance regulations prior to calling in air or artillery strikes on the enemy. Sen. Barry Goldwater felt that the regulations and procedures were shameful and not the air strikes. He said the procedures "had as much to do with our casualties as the enemy themselves."[19]

Former Vietnam prisoner of war and United States senator Jeremiah A. Denton Jr. wrote this concerning U.S. pursuit of the Vietnam War: "But in no other war did any nation lean farther over backward trying to avoid killing innocents than did we—in spite of exceptions such as My Lai."[20] (The My Lai massacre and the whole subject of atrocities by U.S. combat soldiers will be examined in a later chapter.)

I hope the issues of genocide, free fire zones, indiscriminate use of firepower, and civilian casualties have been dealt with in an informative manner. A goal of this book is to help keep these matters in correct perspective.

An incident that occurred during the Tet Offensive of 1968 probably created the longest lasting image of the horror and brutality of the Vietnam War. Vietnamese National Police chief Gen. Nguyen Loc Loan executed Vietcong prisoner Bay Lop in the streets of Saigon by placing a .38 to his head and pulling the trigger. This act was done in the full view of the cameras. The still photograph taken by photographer Eddie Adams was flashed worldwide and won Adams a Pulitzer Prize. The film of the incident was broadcast to 20 million Americans on *The Huntley-Brinkley Report* on February 2, 1968.

This incident had a great impact on U.S. public opinion. A U.S. high school textbook of 1995 describes it this way, accompanied by the famous picture:

> Particularly alarming was the savage flavor that the war had taken on. In the midst of the fighting, television cameras recorded the sight of a captured Vietcong guerrilla being led up

to a South Vietnamese police officer on a downtown Saigon street. The officer pulled out his pistol and shot the young soldier through the head, leaving him lying dead with his blood gushing out onto the street. No single image did more to create a feeling among Americans that Vietnam was an immoral conflict.[21]

This incident does show the horror and brutality of war, but it is examined in this book for another reason. As horrible as the incident was, its brutality then and for the most part up to the present day has been portrayed as unprovoked. What the textbook of today does is repeat the errors of omission that occurred during the reporting of the event at the time.

Photographer Adams later said that he talked to Loan and that Loan said, "They killed many of my men and many of your people."[22] Adams continued referring to the executed Vietcong: "They found out that he was the same guy who killed one of his—uh—Loan's officers and wiped out his whole family."[23] Adams also expressed regret for what the photograph had done to Loan's life.

It seemed to be a truism of the war that U.S. and South Vietnamese actions such as these were banner headlines and even framed in a worse light than they actually were while enemy actions of this nature went unreported. This phenomenon continues through more recent times.

A story in *Time Magazine* in 1993 rehashes the incident, then adds: "A quarter-century later, the victim's widow, Nguyen Than Lop, 60, lives in a decrepit house on the outskirts of what is now called Ho Chi Minh City. For a decade after the war, she and her three children were homeless. The Vietnamese provided shelter only after a Japanese TV crew found her living in a field."[24] A reader of the article cannot escape the message that this is somehow America's fault.

As for the executed Vietcong, the article says: "The fate of

Lop, a captured Viet Cong captain, was a starkly dramatic moment in a nationwide battle that lasted 25 days and was fought in more than 100 cities, towns and military bases."[25] Given all the peripheral information surrounding the mention of Lop, it is interesting that what Lop had done prior to his execution is still omitted.

The picture is shown in the February 15, 1993, issue of *Time* as well as on *Time*'s front cover on April 5, 1993, as part of a cross and bearing the title "The Generation That Forgot God." The picture is also featured in the introductory segment of every videotape in the series *The Vietnam War with Walter Cronkite*. Millions of people have seen the picture, and millions will continue to see it in the future without the slightest idea of the context of circumstances that surrounded the event. These millions will continue to have an incomplete understanding of this brutal image that became an antiwar icon.

Part of the Cronkite series is the episode called "The Tet Offensive." In this segment, the incident of General Loan killing the Vietcong captive is shown in full color. It is narrated by CBS newsman John Lawrence, who says, "The military commander of the operation to secure Saigon, General Nguyen Loc Loan, arrives for an inspection. General Loan gets special attention from the troops. He often leads his national police in action, and last week he showed them just how tough he is by shooting and killing a prisoner in cold blood."[26]

While the circumstances surrounding the incident may or may not have been known with the original broadcast in 1968, they surely were when the series was produced by CBS in 1985. CBS News and Walter Cronkite apparently felt that the circumstances surrounding the event were not relevant information to be recorded in its version of history.

CBS News is not alone in portraying the incident this way. Most accounts of the event portray it as an unprovoked summary execution of a prisoner of war.

There is another image branded into the American mind showing the brutality of the Vietnam War. Similar to the General Loan incident, there is some vital information missing or misconstrued in this second incident also.

In June 1972 Associated Press photographer Nick Ut took a picture of a South Vietnamese girl running naked down a road after she had been severely burned by a napalm strike on her village. This photograph, published worldwide, became a Pulitzer Prize winner also, and similar to the General Loan incident it became symbolic of the brutality and horror of the Vietnam War. It also contributed, wittingly or unwittingly, to a picture of U.S. brutality in the Vietnam War.

CBS News correspondent Bob Simon reported on the incident in 1972, and it also was portrayed in the 1985 videotape series *The Vietnam War with Walter Cronkite*. Original videotape footage from 1972 was narrated by Simon, and in it he said, "Ten-year-old Phan Kim Phuc will never forget the day it rained fire on her village, the day bombers mistakenly dropped napalm on a road where she was playing."[27] The videotape vividly shows the burned little girl running down the road. Kim Phuc is interviewed in person thirteen years later as an adult. What happened to her in the years since the incident is the subject of the story.

In neither incident did CBS News see fit to mention that the napalm dropped on Kim Phuc *was not* dropped by U.S. bombers but accidentally by the South Vietnamese air force. Viewers are left to draw their own conclusion as to what happened and who had caused this tragic occurrence. It is assumed that most Americans then and most people viewing the 1985 videotape in the future will reach the conclusion that it was Americans who dropped that napalm. Was this omission of pertinent facts in 1972 and later in 1985 designed to emphasize particularly the brutality of America's effort in the Vietnam War? If it was for this purpose it most likely has succeeded

169

in accomplishing that goal for the history that most people will be exposed to in the future. Kim Phuc's napalmed picture also appears on every opening interlude of Walter Cronkite's 1985 videotape series.

CBS is not alone in perpetuating the myth that Americans were responsible for this brutal incident. While there are probably many instances where this story has been misconstrued, several examples of conscious or unconscious slanting of the story can be shown.

In 1989 the Associated Press ran an article from Havana, Cuba, quoting from a Kim Phuc interview while she was visiting there. In the interview she is quoted as saying, "If I ever see those pilots who dropped the bombs on me, or any American pilots, I would say to them, the war is over. The past is the past. I would ask those pilots what can they do to bring us together."[28]

Given the wording Kim Phuc uses, the average reader obviously would conclude that American pilots had dropped the napalm. Is this wording consciously or unconsciously trying to elicit this conclusion? Is it possible that this is another in a series of innocent mistakes concerning the incident? Without a question, as the omissions are repeated the mistakes will be perpetuated for history.

Time Magazine made an error in reference to the Kim Phuc incident as late as 1992. In its January 1992 issue a sidebar called "Symbols of War" appeared in the letters to the editor section. *Time* wrote: "On rare occasions a photograph captures the intense emotion of an event so powerfully that it becomes symbolic of that event."[29] Shown in the article are the picture of "a Croat youth crying at the funeral of his father" and the 1972 picture of Kim Phuc and the napalm incident. *Time* explained that the picture of the Croat youth was one of those classic photographs that had this effect on its readers. It then wrote: "Some felt it exemplified the civil war in Yugoslavia in the same way that the 1972 photo of children fleeing an American napalm strike epitomized the horror of the Vietnam conflict."[30]

Time was written a letter by this author correcting them in their error of stating it was an "American" napalm strike. It should have been written accurately that it was an accidental strike by the South Vietnamese air force.

Time responded with a letter to this author admitting its mistake and stating: "We regret the inaccuracy, and we thank you for your help in calling it to our attention. Although we were unable to publish your letter, you can be sure that our files have been corrected."[31]

Who could guess how many millions of people read the original erroneous article? A historical error of great magnitude occurred which perpetuates an inaccurate image of the United States in Vietnam. It possibly could contribute to erroneous history for the future, and *Time* cannot publish a letter that corrects their mistake or publicly correct their own mistake! All should rest easy, however, since *Time* assures us that their "files have been corrected."

In May 1995 *Life Magazine* published a picture of the Kim Phuc incident. Maybe since *Life* and *Time* are published by the same company the evidence of corrected *Time* files was evident in the caption of the picture in the *Life* article. The caption stated: "South Vietnamese aircraft had dropped U.S. napalm near the Buddhist temple where nine-year-old Phan Thi Kim Phuc and her family had been hiding in Trang Bang, a village besieged by the North Vietnamese Army."[32]

It should be noted that *Life* chose to emphasize that the napalm dropped was **U.S napalm.** *Life* should have then in all objectivity and consistency mentioned that the North Vietnamese were besieging Trang Bang with Soviet and Communist Chinese rifles, bullets, and rockets as well. It seems that concerning the Vietnam War many times the reporting at the time and what has been carried into the present distinctly tries to

171

put the U.S. effort into the poorest light. This lack of objectivity will contribute to a perpetuation of an inaccurate historical record concerning that war.

Much of what has been related in this chapter concerning the unique horror of the Vietnam conflict has been somewhat refuted that belief and mind-set. In addition to that, it has been shown that even when the brutal events did occur the story was sometimes misconstrued and even related in a blatantly inaccurate manner. This causes the question to arise as to why this is so. One answer is given by Norman Podhoretz:

> One can easily understand how the young of the 1960s—who in general notoriously deficient in historical knowledge or understanding, and who therefore tended to look upon all the ills around them, including relatively minor ones, as unique in their evil dimension—would genuinely imagine that never in all of human experience had there been anything to compare in cruelty and carnage with the war in Vietnam. But how did it happen that so many of their elders and teachers, who did have historical perspective and had even lived through two earlier and bloodier wars, should have taken so "absurdly unhistorical" a view of Vietnam? The answer is quite simply, that they opposed—or had turned against—the American effort to save South Vietnam from Communism. Being against the end, they could not tolerate the very means whose earlier employment in Korea and World War II they had not only accepted but applauded.[33]

Added to this is what has been stated previously, that those young who were against the war at the time had a vested interest in perpetuating the evil and horrendous nature of the war and the U.S. role in it to reinforce and exonerate the position they took at the time of the war. The effect is a cloudy and inaccurate picture of the war, which is being perpetuated for history.

172

Notes

1. Harry G. Summers Jr., "Deliberate Distortions Still Obscure Understanding of the Vietnam War. It's Time They Were Laid to Rest," *Vietnam Magazine,* August 1989, p. 58.
2. A. Francis Hatch, "One Despicable Legacy of the Vietnam War Is the False Portrayal of American Soldiers as Bloodthirsty Barbarians," *Vietnam Magazine,* August 1995, p. 58.
3. Harry G. Summers, *Vietnam War Almanac* (New York: Facts on File, 1985), p. 229.
4. Summers, "Deliberate Distortions," p. 58.
5. Stanley Karnow, *Vietnam, a History* (New York: Viking, 1983), p. 653.
6. John M. Blum, ed., *The National Experience, a History of the United States* (Fort Worth, TX: Harcourt, Brace, and Jovanovich, 1993), p. 871.
7. Carol Berkin et al., *American Voices, a History of the United States* (Glenview, IL: Scott Foresman, 1995), p. 749.
8. Karnow, *Vietnam,* p. 653.
9. Videotape, *The Vietnam War with Walter Cronkite,* "Fire from the Sky" (New York: CBS News, 1985).
10. Summers, *Vietnam War Almanac,* p. 100.
11. Ibid.
12. Jacksel M. Broughton, "Wasted Air Power," *Vietnam Magazine,* August 1994, p. 18.
13. Ibid.
14. Summers, *Vietnam War Almanac,* p. 173.
15. Daniel Ellsberg, *War Crimes and the American Conscience,* p. 83, quoted in Norman Podhoretz, *Why We Were in Vietnam* (New York: Simon and Schuster, 1982), p. 186.
16. Podhoretz, *Why Were We in Vietnam,* pp. 186–87.
17. Guenter Lewy, *America in Vietnam* (New York: Oxford University Press, 1978), pp. 304 and 448, as quoted in ibid., p. 187.
18. Roger Hilsman, *To Move a Nation* (New York: Doubleday, 1967), p. 444, as quoted in Lewy, *America in Vietnam,* p. 303.
19. Lewy, *America in Vietnam,* p. 303.
20. Jeremiah A. Denton Jr., "The U.S. Must Maintain Cold War Principles," in David L. Bender, *The Vietnam War Opposing Viewpoints* (St. Paul, MN: Greenhaven, 1984), p. 130.
21. Berkin et al., *American Voices,* pp. 740–41.
22. Eddie Adams in William Stearnman, videotape, *Television's Vietnam* (Washington, DC: Accuracy in Media, 1985).
23. Ibid.

24. Richard Hornik, "Good Morning Vietnam," *Time Magazine,* February 15, 1993, p. 42.
25. Ibid.
26. John Lawrence in *The Vietnam War with Walter Cronkite,* "The Tet Offensive" (New York: CBS News, 1985).
27. Bob Simon in *The Vietnam War with Walter Cronkite,* "Legacies."
28. "Napalmed Vietnamese Girl Reunited with Photographer," *Herald-Palladium,* Benton Harbor–St. Joseph, Michigan, Monday, August 21, 1989.
29. "Letters to the Editor," *Time Magazine,* January 6, 1993, p. 15.
30. Ibid.
31. Patrick Smith in a letter to James M. Griffiths, March 5, 1992.
32. Janet Mason, "Caught in Time," *Life Magazine,* May, 1995, p. 44.
33. Podhoretz, *Why We Were in Vietnam,* p. 193.

10

"Lost War"

If the question were to be posed to a great number of Americans if the United States won or lost the war in Vietnam it is assumed that many, if not most, would answer that the United States did lose the war. This in part is attributable to the sources that are used as historical reference for the war. These sources have seemingly decided to emphasize the terms *lose* and *lost war* for posterity when describing the Vietnam War.

For the person who is seeking deeper historical understanding of the Vietnam War it is necessary to examine more deeply the term *lost war* as it applies to the Vietnam War. Did the United States "lose" the Vietnam War in the generally assumed meaning of losing a war, or is this another instance of the whole story not being told? It will be the purpose of this chapter to explore some of the information surrounding this question.

Examples of the use of the *lost war* terminology abound, and surely most readers have experienced this description at one time or another. It is necessary to cite only a few examples of this use to illustrate the point.

In the initial videotape in Walter Cronkite's videotape series about the Vietnam War the famous newscaster illustrates the point. In the resonating voice possessed only by Cronkite he says, "If you look back at the Vietnam War, you can find a few decisions that shaped the course of history and led the United States slowly into the only war we ever lost."[1] Walter

Cronkite was a source of credibility to at least a generation of Americans. If Cronkite uttered the words *lost war,* then surely to most people lost war was what it must have been.

U.S. high school textbooks of 1995 echo the lost war theme. *These United States, the Questions of Our Past* states in reference to Vietnam: "It was the first war that America had lost, and it undermined the nation's confidence in itself."[2]

Another U.S. high school textbook, *American Voices, a History of the United States, 1865 to the Present,* states it more emphatically: "It had been the longest war in American history, and it was now the only conflict the United States had ever clearly lost."[3] The reader should note the inclusion of the *clearly lost* terminology in this particular textbook.

Channel One is a daily news broadcast that is beamed via satellite and shown in thousands of schools across the United States. Millions of U.S. students in middle school and high school watch these broadcasts as a source of educational information.

On May 18, 1992, *Channel One* aired a report concerning Vietnam by Anderson Cooper. Reporter Cooper stated reasons given at that time for the United States refusing to normalize relations with Vietnam. Among the reasons were human rights violations by the Vietnamese against the people living there, the 1978 Vietnamese invasion of Cambodia, and Vietnam not adequately accounting for U.S. troops still listed as missing in action from the war. Cooper also said U.S. nonrecognition of Vietnam was caused by another factor, "the unstated reason, a reluctance to recognize a country that defeated the U.S. in war."[4]

Earlier in the broadcast Anderson Cooper had uttered these words: "Ever since American combat troops were driven out in 1973, few Americans have seen Vietnam."[5] The reader should note that Channel One and reporter Anderson Cooper consciously or unconsciously gave a report that conjured an image of U.S. combat forces being militarily driven out of Vietnam. It would be very easy for impressionable teenagers of the 1990s to perceive from this report a militarily defeated U.S. military hastily fleeing from defeat in a lost war.

It also would be easy for history to record from Walter Cronkite's videotape and the U.S. textbooks that the United States had been militarily defeated and had lost a war in the classic sense of *lost war* understanding. For this reason further analysis is necessary.

First and foremost the scenario surrounding the exit of U.S. combat forces did not even remotely resemble being driven out militarily. U.S. troops had been withdrawn in an orderly, incremental fashion from a high of 550,000 in 1969 to a low of 24,000 at the end of 1972. These troops departed in an orderly incremental fashion as troops were removed in stages up until the final withdrawal. These forces were withdrawn as it was deemed that the South Vietnamese possessed the ability to take over the combat role that the United States had performed.

U.S. forces departed Vietnam in March of 1973 after a cease-fire and a peace agreement had been signed. One of the premises of the peace agreement signed by the North Vietnamese agreed to the preservation of the right of South Vietnam's continued existence. There was no military defeat of U.S. combat forces or surrender similar to the defeat of the French at Dien Bien Phu in 1954. Any defeat in Vietnam was of the South Vietnamese by the North Vietnamese in 1975. The war was lost in 1975, two full years after the United States had marched out of Vietnam. It was lost by the South Vietnamese, not the United States of America. It is difficult to imagine a country losing a war, in the usually accepted sense, when that country was not present in the country when it was conquered. So much for saying the United States lost the war in Vietnam if generally accepted standards of losing a war are applied.

177

Battlefield defeat is what we suffered at Bataan and Corregidor in 1942, when General Jonathan M. Wainwright surrendered his command to the Japanese. Battlefield defeat was what we suffered during the Battle of the Bulge in 1944, when the 422nd and 432nd Infantry regiments of the U.S. 106th Infantry Division surrendered to the German attackers. Battlefield defeat was what the U.S. Eighth Army and X Corps suffered in November 1950, as the Chinese armies forced us out of North Korea. And battlefield defeat was what the Army of the Republic of Vietnam suffered in April 1975, when the North Vietnamese blitzkrieg rolled south.

Nothing even remotely similar happened to the U.S. military in Vietnam.[6]

Not only was the United States not present militarily when the decisive battles ending the Vietnam War were waged; the United States was never defeated by enemy forces in any major engagement while it was participating in combat in Vietnam.

In October of 1965 the first engagement between North Vietnamese Regulars and U.S. forces took place in the Ia Drang Valley. U.S. forces killed nearly two thousand enemy men while losing about three hundred. The enemy was sent scurrying back into its sanctuaries in Cambodia after breaking contact with the U.S. forces.

Tet in 1968 was a massive defeat for enemy forces, as has been discussed previously, and the enemy was massively defeated again in the Eastertide Offensive of 1972. By the time of this engagement most U.S. combat forces had already been withdrawn and airpower was used to thwart the North Vietnamese, costing them approximately one hundred thousand casualties.

Many people have elevated North Vietnamese military commander Vo Nguyen Giap to the status of military genius for engineering communist strategy during the war. It is hard to understand this phenomenon considering the massive defeats that he took when he challenged U.S. military might. Giap's brilliant strategy appeared to be that of sending his men to be sacrificed as in a meat grinder. Military genius should be judged not on the basis of how many of a general's own men he is willing to sacrifice but on how many of the enemy he can manage to eliminate. "In 1969, Giap admitted that from 1964 to 1969 alone he lost 500,000 soldiers killed on the battlefield, and an untold number of wounded or missing. This evidence challenges the myth of invincibility that has surrounded General Giap."[7]

Not only were U.S. forces not defeated by a guerrilla enemy, neither were they driven from Vietnam by military force. In 1969, six years before the end of the war, the 3rd Marine Division and most of the Army's 9th Infantry Division left Vietnam. Their withdrawal was prompted by political considerations at home, not battlefield conditions in Vietnam. These withdrawals continued apace, and by mid-1972, almost three years before the end of the war, all U.S. ground forces had left the country. U.S. air and naval forces were also phased down and in January 1973 (over two years before the fall of Saigon) all military forces were completely withdrawn.

As earlier articles in this magazine [*Vietnam Magazine*] have emphasized, the American military was not defeated by North Vietnam's final 1975 blitzkrieg for the simple reason that there were no American military forces there to be defeated. They had left the country years earlier. Ironically that irrefutable historical fact does not seem to have registered on many Americans who still talk about America's military defeat in Vietnam. They are entitled to their own set of opinions but, as former Secretary of Defense James Schlesinger once observed, they are not entitled to their own set of facts.[8]

Many analysts are beginning to come to the conclusion

that the U.S. military effort was more successful than previously thought. "Despite all the blunders, a number of historians and military specialists are coming to the conclusion that the American military effort in Vietnam was more successful than was recognized at the time."[9]

Included with these historians is George C. Herring. "Professor Herring at the University of Kentucky has suggested that 'the ultimate irony' of the war may be that the American position in South Vietnam was stronger at the end of 1972, just before the Paris peace agreement, than at any previous point in the war."[10] Samuel L. Popkin, who has been an associate professor of political science at Harvard and the University of California at San Diego, has concurred. "Mr. Popkin concurs and adds, 'There's no doubt that if Nixon had kept up U.S. aid after 1973, South Vietnam might have survived.'"[11]

Troung Nhu Tang echoed the same assessment from the other side. The former Vietcong minister of justice, referring to 1972, said: "Indeed in strictly military terms it was increasingly evident that American arms were again scoring victories, just as they had during Tet, in Cambodia, and in so many of the pitched battles in which they confronted Vietcong and North Vietnamese main forces."[12] Richard Nixon added: "After their decisive defeat on the ground in the spring offensive and the destruction of their war-making capabilities by the December bombing, the North Vietnamese knew that militarily they were up against almost impossible odds."[13]

The foregoing evidence should shed light to the reader on the lost war thesis. U.S. forces were never defeated in a major battle in Vietnam. This makes it difficult to categorize the war as a military loss. In fact, the major military encounters that occurred were military victories for U.S., forces. These forces were not driven out militarily by any means either. America's position in South Vietnam was said to be at its strongest point in 1972. Military withdrawal took place in an orderly fashion after a negotiated peace settlement, which included South Vietnam's guaranteed right to exist, was signed. Finally, when North Vietnam conquered the South it was at least two full years after the United States had withdrawn its combat forces.

The type of scenario that surrounded the collapse of South Vietnam surely does not conjure up images of the generally understood meaning of the United States losing a war. Describing Vietnam as a lost war for the United States surely does not take into account a full disclosure of the circumstances as they were.

Along the same lines, the most recently released casualty figures in the Vietnam War also belie the notion that the United States lost the war. These figures show that the enemy suffered massive casualties during the war. In an Associated Press article from Hanoi it is stated: "Twenty years after the end of the Vietnam War, the government disclosed Monday that 1.1 million Communist fighters died and 600,000 were wounded in 21 years of conflict. . . . Previous estimates in the West said the Communist forces lost about 666,000 fighters. During the war, North Vietnam played down its losses to boost morale at home and discourage South Vietnam and the United States. . . . Nearly 58,200 U.S. soldiers were killed and 223,748 South Vietnamese died."[14] A great disparity in kill ratio such as this undermines the credibility of those who assert that the United States lost the Vietnam War.

One concept that did go down to defeat during the Vietnam War was the concept of "People's War." Many people entertained and still entertain the romanticized notion of the noble peasant guerrilla defeating the industrialized, imperialistic, and militaristic superpower through guerrilla war. This also did not occur.

In the early 1960s the Soviet Union envisioned wars of national liberation as the wave of the future. Communist Chinese theory called these People's Wars, and they were to result in

defeat of colonialist, industrialized powers by guerrillas indigenous to the country. Many portrayed the Vietnam war as an example of this type of struggle with the peasant Vietcong taking
on the superpower United States. As has been established earlier in this book, the Vietcong were decimated by 1970 and the
bulk of the fighting and ultimate North Vietnamese victory
were by conventional regular army forces of the North, not by
any guerrilla in black pajamas fighting a so-called People's
War. If any war was clearly lost it was the People's War.

An alternative method of looking at the Vietnam War is to
view the war as not an end unto itself but as a part of the overall
struggle referred to as the cold war. When this perspective is
used, U.S. participation in the Vietnam War is viewed in a much
more positive light than has been the norm.

The argument advanced is that the American participation in the Vietnam War helped to defeat international communism and pave the way for the ultimate collapse of America's
chief adversary in the cold war, the Soviet Union. The U.S. side
won the cold war. Even if it is perceived that the United States
had a setback in Vietnam, it did not compromise the overall
aim of defeating world communism.

Others feel that by fighting the communists in Vietnam
the United States bought time for other Southeast Asian nations to bolster themselves against possible communist insurgencies. It can be assumed, in retrospect, that given its
financial situation the Soviet Union could ill afford to fund the
increasing military needs of North Vietnam as the war escalated. If this was true, other potential communist insurgencies
in Southeast Asia probably had to do without Soviet assistance, thereby gaining time for the noncommunist forces in
other countries to bolster their positions.

Many have said that the United States spent the Soviet
Union into oblivion. The war in Vietnam can be viewed as part
of this process.

Former secretary of state Dean Rusk, national security adviser Walt Rostow, and prime minister of Singapore Lee Kuan Yew, commenting on whether the high costs of the Vietnam War were justified, give an answer in the affirmative.

Dean Rusk, Walt Rostow, Lee Kwan Yew, and many other geopoliticians across the globe to this day answer yes. They conclude that without U.S. intervention in Vietnam, Communist hegemony—both Soviet and Chinese—would have spread farther through South and East Asia to include Indonesia, Thailand, and possibly India. Some would go further and say that the USSR would have been led to take greater risks to extend its influence elsewhere in the world, particularly in the Middle East where it might well have sought control of the oil-producing nations.[15]

Richard Armitage, a former assistant secretary of defense, supports the belief that U.S. Vietnam involvement bought time for other nations to resist communism: "Arguably, the non-Communist nations of Asia have thrived, and this has been so because of the time bought for them by the sacrifice of our nation and our people."[16]

Former secretary of state Henry Kissinger echoed the same theme: "America failed in Vietnam, but it gave the other nations of Southeast Asia time to deal with their own insurrections."[17]

Former British prime minister Margaret Thatcher was complimentary to the United States while supporting the same concept of the previous luminaries. In a speech, "Thatcher commended Americans for their involvement in the Vietnam War, saying that the offensive saved many other countries from communist rule."[18]

Some present-day media commentators have chosen to place the Vietnam War into the context of the cold war also. Media commentators in general have rarely portrayed the effort in Vietnam in a positive light, but ABC News commentator Jack Smith has said this about the war: "Containment, my friends, worked. We won the cold war. And however meaningless Vietnam seemed at the time, it contributed to the fall of communism."[19]

George Will, syndicated columnist and ABC News commentator, said on *This Week with David Brinkley* on April 30, 1995 (the twentieth anniversary of the fall of Saigon), "I think the final judgment on Vietnam has yet to be written. It seems to me that it was part of the cold war and we won the cold war and maybe it contributed."[20]

Harry Summers Jr. eloquently stated the case concerning the linking of the Vietnam War, the cold war, the struggle for democracy, and the concept of lost war:

> When Saigon fell, it was seen as a plus for communism and as a loss for democracy and the United States. But Vietnam was just a battle in a much larger war, and the final victory of that war is now at hand. With the fall of the Berlin Wall and the breakup of the Soviet Union, it is Communism that finds itself on the ash heap of history. And it is democracy, and the United States, that has emerged as the ultimate victor in that epic struggle.[21]

Summers also said in reference to the Vietnam Veterans Memorial:

> Ten years ago, they called it a "Black Gash of Shame," a "Hole in the Ground," a "Sarcophagus." The one thing that it was never called was a "Victory Monument." But as history continued to unfold, that's what it has turned out to be. . . .
> It is a world profoundly different from the one when the

Vietnam Veterans Memorial was dedicated. And it is different in large measure because of the sacrifices made by those whose names are inscribed on the Wall. "Black Gash of Shame" indeed. How about "V" for victory instead?[22]

From the foregoing the reader no doubt has been able to ascertain that the concept of the Vietnam War being a clear-cut loss for the United States does not command unanimity of opinion. Evidence suggests and the case has been eloquently stated that to many the war was a victory of sorts.

One last issue needs to be examined before departing the lost war question, and that is the question of double standard. It can be asserted that performance in the Vietnam War was evaluated by a different standard than other relatively recent military engagements such as Korea and even Desert Storm. Analysis here is in no way intended to diminish the valiant efforts of U.S. fighting forces in these two engagements. It is simply designed to show that a type of double standard exists in judging these efforts and the effort in Vietnam.

During the latter years of the Vietnam War a growing consensus of opinion in the United States was that we had done enough to defend South Vietnam. It was felt that if the South Vietnamese could not defend themselves after all our effort then they would just have to suffer the consequences. Accordingly we removed all our troops as part of the Paris Peace Agreements in 1973. The United States did not remain to enforce the peace agreement.

Not only would the United States not commit ground forces to the defense of South Vietnam, but a series of congressional decisions including the Case-Church Amendment and the War Powers Act would prevent Presidents Richard Nixon and Gerald Ford from enforcing the peace agreement with airpower or even extending military aid to the South.

North Vietnam sized up the situation, violated the peace

agreement, and invaded South Vietnam knowing full well that the U.S. Congress would forbid retaliatory action. The result was the conquest of South Vietnam.

In Korea an armistice was signed in 1953 and the United States remained pledged to the defense of South Korea. U.S. ground troops remained in Korea. As of 1996 there are still 40,000 U.S. ground troops still stationed in South Korea that would act as a tripwire if North Korea attempted an invasion. These troops most likely would not be able to repel a ground invasion, so it is implicit that the full force of U.S. airpower would be brought to bear if North Korea invaded.

There has not been talk about whether South Korea, like South Vietnam, should stand on its own feet and be able to defend itself after all the aid the United States has extended to them. This is the situation even after more than forty years of U.S. assistance. The result is that South Korea still exists as a country and the Korean War is not considered a lost war.

Readers should consider what the result most likely would have been in Vietnam if the United States had left 40,000 troops and the implicit threat of U.S. airpower to enforce the Paris Peace Accord. Would South Vietnam have fallen and the Vietnam War been labeled as lost under these circumstances? Not likely!

In 1991 Saddam Hussein's Iraqi forces that had invaded Kuwait were driven out of Kuwait and soundly defeated by coalition forces spearheaded by the United States in Operation Desert Storm. The war-making power of Hussein was destroyed, and to the present day his country, Iraq, is under constant monitoring and surveillance by UN inspectors and allied air flights.

Desert Storm has been heralded as a great U.S. military victory, and surely it was to the credit of the United States. There was a cease fire and an agreement signed to end hostilities. In this case, as in Korea, there remains a credible military threat to Saddam Hussein if he attempts any aggressive moves. Kuwait remains liberated and Saddam Hussein defanged.

It is a foregone conclusion that without military enforcement of the agreements after Desert Storm, Saddam Hussein would most likely engage in aggressive military moves against his neighbors. With the military enforcement and threat Hussein dares not make a move. Such a military monitoring and threat did not exist to enforce the Paris Peace Accords concerning Vietnam.

What would have happened in Korea or the Middle East after Desert Storm if there had not been credible military enforcement of agreements made? Hypothetically, what would it mean if the United States had removed its military deterrent in Korea and the Persian Gulf regions? Would liberated and previously defended countries have fallen victim to aggressive conquerors? Would Korea and Desert Storm then have become lost wars?

Vietnam fell to the communists after the United States removed its combat troops and effectively removed the deterrent of U.S. airpower. The Vietnam War is considered a lost war by many. Why was a different standard applied to the U.S. effort in Vietnam? If the war was lost, it was the result of not enforcing the peace as occurred in the other situations.

Could it be said that the final decision of won or lost is not in on Korea or Desert Storm? To judge using Vietnam standards the final decision will not be made until U.S. military force is removed in these areas and it is observed if the formerly defended areas are conquered or not.

I hope this chapter has provoked some thought considering the lost war question. Minimally it is hoped that a different perspective of the lost war concept has been presented and the reader will be better able to judge the validity of the lost war label as it applies to the Vietnam War.

187

Notes

1. Videotape, *The Vietnam War with Walter Cronkite,* "The Seeds of Conflict," New York, CBS News, 1987.
2. Irwin Unger, *These United States, the Questions of Our Past* (Englewood Cliffs, NJ: Prentice Hall, 1995), p. 856.
3. Carol Berkin et al., *American Voices, a History of the United States, 1865 to the Present* (Glenview, IL: Scott Foresman, 1995), p. 750.
4. Anderson Cooper, *Channel One,* Whittle Communications, 1992.
5. Ibid.
6. Harry G. Summers Jr., "While the United States Was Not Defeated in Battle, Our Allies Still Pay the Bitter Cost of Abandonment," *Vietnam Magazine,* June 1995, p. 6.
7. Harry G. Summers, Jr., "Deliberate Distortions Still Obscure Understanding of the Vietnam War. It's Time They Were Laid to Rest," *Vietnam Magazine,* August 1989, p. 59.
8. Ibid.
9. Fox Butterfield, "The New Vietnam Scholarship," *New York Times Magazine,* February 1983, p. 56.
10. George C. Herring, *America's Longest War,* in ibid., p. 58.
11. Samuel L. Popkin in Butterfield, "The New Vietnam Scholarship," p. 58.
12. Troung Nhu Tang, *A Vietcong Memoir, an Inside Account of the Vietnam War and Its Aftermath* (New York: Vintage, 1985), p. 211.
13. Richard Nixon, *The Real War* (New York: Warner, 1980), p. 113.
14. "Viets Say War Deaths Over One Million," *Herald-Palladium,* Benton Harbor–St. Joseph, Michigan, April 4, 1995.
15. Robert S. McNamara, *In Retrospect, the Tragedy and Lessons of Vietnam* (New York: Random House, 1995), p. 319.
16. Richard Armitage in Bill McCloud, *What Should We Tell Our Children About Vietnam?* (Norman: University of Oklahoma Press, 1989), p. 5.
17. Henry Kissinger in McCloud, *What Should We Tell Our Children about Vietnam?,* p. 69.
18. Margaret Thatcher in a speech to the Economics Club of Southwestern Michigan, *Herald-Palladium,* St. Joseph–Benton Harbor, Michigan, January 24, 1992.
19. Jack Smith in Jan Scruggs, ed., *Writings on the Wall, Reflections on the Vietnam Veterans Memorial* (Washington, DC: Vietnam Veterans Memorial Fund, 1994), p. 15.
20. George Will on ABC News, *This Week with David Brinkley,* April 30, 1995.
21. Harry Summers Jr., in Scruggs, *Writings on the Wall,* p. 42.
22. Ibid., pp. 41–42.

11

Maligned Warriors

Earlier in this book it was asserted that historically U.S. efforts in wars were most likely to be portrayed in highly favorable terms. This treatment, it also was asserted, ceased with the Vietnam War. In fact, it has been the perspective of this book to say that just the opposite happened with the Vietnam War. Participation in the Vietnam War probably has been most likely portrayed in a less favorable light than reality would dictate.

Similarly, this phenomenon can be applied to the warriors of the Vietnam War. Never before have U.S. fighting forces been so maligned as was, and continues to be in some instances, the Vietnam veteran.

Most readers have been exposed to a very positive image of the U.S. GI in most of America's wars. Examples such as Gary Cooper's portrayal of Sergeant York in World War I and the variety of roles played by John Wayne in movies about World War II and Korea displayed a very favorable image of U.S. fighting men. The image of the rock solid, highly moral American fighting man prevailed. He loved children in the villages that he liberated, and he was a conquering hero who passed out chocolate and treated the indigenous people with utmost respect the vast majority of the time.

Simultaneously, most movies portrayed America's enemies as vicious, incompetent,and bumbling idiots. Enemy troops constantly were easily outfoxed and outfought by the wily Americans.

Vietnam veterans grew up with this image of the American fighting man and in turn were portrayed as the antithesis of this image. Americans in the Vietnam war have been portrayed as vicious, immoral, and at times bumbling idiots who were outfoxed and outfought by the wily enemy. Nearly every conceivable malady has been attributed to the warriors of the Vietnam War.

These images of the American soldier in Vietnam will be examined and analyzed in this chapter. What the images were and at times still are will be discussed. Differing points of view as to the validity of these images will also be examined. The reader I hope will be enabled to make an informed judgment concerning the correct image of the Vietnam veteran.

The image of the Vietnam War and the soldiers who participated in it will probably be passed on to future generations through video more than any other category of communication. This media includes both the documentary type that has been done by various news sources, including U.S. network news and the Public Broadcasting System (PBS), and the Hollywood version of the war.

Hollywood has contributed and most likely will continue to contribute its version of the Vietnam War with movies such as *Platoon, Full Metal Jacket, Born on the Fourth of July, Hamburger Hill, The Deer Hunter,* and a host of others.

Most likely the war will become in history what these movies have portrayed it to be. Similarly, the image of the U.S. soldier in Vietnam will be recorded for posterity the way it appeared in these movies.

Platoon is arguably the most familiar film about the Vietnam War. Oliver Stone's Academy Award winner depicts an infantry platoon that operates near the Cambodian border in 1967. This movie serves to illustrate events that surely occurred at various places at various times in the long Vietnam War. A great variety of cliché-like incidents occur to this particular platoon that make it a microcosm of the entire Vietnam War. Seemingly anything that ever occurred in that war occurred in that platoon. Examples of poor morale, malingering, U.S. soldiers fighting and killing each other, dope smoking, and atrocities such as rape and murder of civilians all make their appearance.

This platoon even has the unusual occurrence of being overrun by the enemy. It becomes more unusual when this platoon called an air strike on their own position and some of them survived the air strike. These occurrences are not unheard of but very unusual. This platoon was very unusual.

Columnist Jeffrey Hart described the portrayal of American soldiers in *Platoon:* "We have endless footage of American soldiers being blown up by an invincible enemy. The soldiers are sloppy, demoralized, pot-smoking. For them, fragging, that is, murdering an officer, is no big deal."[1]

Ron Kovic, the marine portrayed in the film *Born on the Fourth of July,* killed a fellow marine accidentally and reported it to his superiors. According to the film, an authorized version of a true story, superior officers never even investigated the incident.

Stanley Kubrick's *Full Metal Jacket* depicts the Tet Offensive in the old imperial capital of Hue. In Kubrick's version of what happened in Hue, one female Vietcong sniper singlehandedly holds off an amazing number of troops of the U.S. Marine Corps.

In addition to these movies, network media have done specials that have carried negative images of the Vietnam veteran long after the war was over.

Among the more outrageous examples was a 1988 CBS News special *The Wall Within,* now used in our schools to teach the "truth" about Vietnam.

Narrated by Dan Rather, a former Marine and well-regarded Vietnam War correspondent who should have known better, it chronicled three Vietnam vets who were supposedly so traumatized by the war that they had taken refuge in the woods of Washington state. One, Terry Bradley, shown howling at the sky, claimed to have skinned alive up to 50 men, women, and babies.[2]

It is not necessary to belabor the point. Most likely readers of this book know full well the stereotypical image of the Vietnam veteran as portrayed by Hollywood and the broadcast media in most cases. The films and news special cited here are only a small, representative sample of the media that abound portraying Vietnam veterans in a negative light.

These same negative stereotypes are being perpetuated by textbooks and other books directed at youth of the 1990s. The pattern is very similar.

In a book directed at younger American readers, *Three Faces of Vietnam,* author Richard L. Wormser offers some incriminating thoughts from a U.S. soldier. The soldier is John Young, who was a prisoner of war taken by the enemy. Wormser writes:

Young expected to be killed or at least tortured. Instead his wounds were attended to and he received sufficient food to keep his strength up. One of the things that went through Young's mind at the time was what he would have done if Vietnamese had been prisoners of his. "I probably would have beat the hell out of them or shot them." He remembered the bombings of Vietnamese villages, the forcible removal of civilians from their homes, the torture of suspected guerrillas, and the mutilations of Vietnamese dead by American soldiers.[3]

To a young, impressionable reader the contrast between the enemy and the U.S. soldier is staggering. John Young had been in Vietnam six weeks before he was captured.

One example of the description of the U.S. soldier in the Vietnam War by an American high school textbook of the 1990s occurs in *These United States, the Questions of Our Past:* "They disobeyed orders or 'fragged' officers by rolling live hand grenades into their tents while they slept. Others turned to drugs to make the time till their tour of duty ended pass more quickly."[4]

Todd & Curti's The American Nation says this about Vietnam veterans: "Thousands of Vietnam veterans turned to drugs or failed to kick the drug habits they had developed during the war. Many others had trouble finding jobs or settling down and starting families. Recent estimates indicate that between 250,000 and 350,000 homeless Americans are Vietnam veterans."[5]

Another high school textbook, *The National Experience, a History of the United States* put things this way: "By 1970 some soldiers were wearing peace symbols and refusing to go into combat. The use of marijuana was general, and, according to estimates, 10 to 15 percent of the troops were addicted to heroin. 'Fragging'—the use of fragmentation grenades to kill unpopular officers—was not unknown."[6]

The same text also states that "both sides in the Vietnam War were guilty of wanton violence, but the disclosure that American soldiers had massacred more than 100 unarmed Vietnamese civilians at My Lai in March 1968 made war atrocities a national issue."[7]

The My Lai massacre, an infamous and notorious event of the Vietnam War, will serve as the turning point in perspective in this chapter. My Lai was terrible and inexcusable and in no way can be condoned. It also cannot be denied. It is a fact and a terrible blemish on U.S. involvement in Vietnam.

My Lai also serves to illustrate how an event can be extrapolated to apply to a whole war and millions of U.S. fighting men who served in that war. The time has come to put My Lai and other events that define the Vietnam veteran in proper perspective.

My Lai, which has also been referred to as Son My, at times has been portrayed as the norm as opposed to an aberration. "Was the My Lai massacre characteristic of the way all 'search and destroy' missions were carried out? Some said that it was. For example, the psychiatrist Robert Jay Lifton, a well known antiwar activist, declared: 'My Lai epitomizes the Vietnam War . . . because every returning soldier can tell of similar incidents, if on a somewhat smaller scale . . .'"[8]

"Three other psychiatrists agreed: *The most important fact about the My Lai massacre is that it was only a minor step beyond the standard, official, routine U.S. policy in Vietnam.*'"[9] "And Hans J. Morgenthau was 'firmly convinced that what happened in My Lai and elsewhere were not accidents, or deviations . . ., but the inevitable outgrowth of the kind of war we were waging.'"[10]

> Yet no evidence existed at the time—and none has materialized since—to substantiate the charge that My Lai was typical. Nor is it likely, given the number of antiwar journalists reporting on Vietnam, that if other atrocities had occurred, they could have been kept secret. Telford Taylor, who had been a prosecutor at Nuremberg and was a strong opponent of the war, disputed the judgment of Lifton and others on this point:[11] "It has been said that the massacre at Son My was not unique, but I am unaware of any evidence of other incidents of comparable magnitude, and the reported reaction of some of the soldiers at Son My strongly indicates that they regarded it as out of the ordinary."[12]

Daniel Ellsberg, himself staunchly antiwar, even understood full well that My Lai was not typical of actions by U.S. soldiers in the Vietnam War:

My Lai was beyond the bounds of permissible behavior, and

194

that is recognizable by virtually every soldier in Vietnam. They know it was wrong: No shots had been fired at the soldiers, no enemy troops were in the village, nobody was armed. The men who were at My Lai knew there were aspects out of the ordinary. That is why they tried to hide the event, talked about it to no one, discussed it very little even among themselves.[13]

My Lai, as has been mentioned before, was a terrible incident in the U.S. record in Vietnam. It was not, however, the norm in that war. Those who have extrapolated this terrible incident unto the backs of millions of U.S. soldiers that served in Vietnam have committed a grave injustice to these warriors. "Facts aside, the public perception that My Lai was a common occurrence was generated largely by the vitriolic assertions and activities of celebrated leaders of the antiwar movement."[14]

It became commonplace to expose so-called American war crimes in Vietnam without substantial unbiased verification of the allegations. What Guenter Lewy calls a "veritable industry of publicizing alleged war crimes"[15] occurred internationally and in the United States itself.

One of these kangaroo courts was the *International War Crimes Tribunal,* organized by Bertrand Russell. This conference was convened with the presumption of guilt rather than innocence. "This assumption of guilt before trial was further strengthened by the membership of the tribunal, which was made up entirely of such outspoken supporters of North Vietnam as Jean-Paul Sartre, Stokely Carmichael, Dave Dellinger, and Isaac Deutscher."[16] Not surprisingly, as Lewy pointed out, the proceedings "relied on evidence supplied by VC/NVA sources or collected in North Vietnam by persons closely aligned with the Communist camp."[17]

A book, *War Crimes and the American Conscience,* emerged from this conference, and its accusatory rhetoric needs to be judged by the validity and jurisprudence of the proceeding itself.

> Of course such conferences and tribunals were not courts of law and were bound by no rules other than those they themselves decided upon; in that sense they had a "right" to do what they did. Nevertheless, in exercising that right, they freely defamed and slandered individuals and groups on the basis of false or faulty evidence, and witnesses of dubious credibility, in proceedings presided over by biased judges.[18]

This conference convened not to ascertain whether Americans were committing war crimes but to prove a preconceived notion that they were. In the mind's eye of the conferees they accomplished their purpose.

While Russell's tribunal was international, similar enterprises were occurring in the United States. One organization that was involved in these activities was Vietnam Veterans Against the War (VVAW). This group held hearings all over the country. "At one of these hearings, in Detroit in 1971, more than a hundred veterans were reported to have testified to 'war crimes which they either committed or witnessed.'"[19]

> Senator Mark Hatfield inserted the transcript into the Congressional Record and demanded an investigation of the charges by the Naval Investigative Service (since mostly marines had been involved). This investigation yielded the following: a refusal by many of the witnesses to be interviewed (despite assurances that they would not be questioned about atrocities they themselves might have committed); inability on the part of one witness to provide details of the atrocities he had described at the Detroit hearings; and "sworn statements of several veterans, corroborated by witnesses"[20] that they had not even attended the hearings at which they had allegedly testified.[21]

The VVAW testimony appears to have about as much validity as the characters highlighted on the CBS special *The Wall Within,* mentioned earlier, aired in 1988 and reported by Dan Rather. This was the story of Vietnam veterans so traumatized by the horror of the war that they were living in the forests of Washington State.

One of the characters was Terry Bradley, who was attributed during the special with having skinned alive fifty Vietnamese, including men, women, and children. Investigation has determined that

> Terry Bradley's military career was marked by misconduct. In 3 1/2 years of service as an Army artilleryman, Bradley compiled a total of 300 days either AWOL or in confinement. There is no record of large numbers of civilians killed near Bradley's unit, which was stationed outside Saigon during his one year tour of duty. In the documentary, Rather acknowledges that Bradley had been diagnosed as a paranoid-schizophrenic . . . Yet Rather praised Bradley as a "truth teller."
>
> Two of the other featured vets had been security guards, not "grunts" exposed to heavy combat. Another claimed to have been traumatized by the loss of a friend in Vietnam in a grisly propeller accident on an aircraft carrier. Now he admits the accident occurred during training off California. Despite these discrepancies, CBS says it stands by its documentary.[22]

Reality diverges from the picture painted concerning war crimes in the Vietnam War. "Contrary to the antiwar movement's charges of a 'war crimes industry,' atrocities by American forces were the exception, and those accused of such offenses were brought to trial. From 1965 to 1973, 201 Army personnel and 77 Marines were court-martialed for serious crimes against Vietnamese civilians."[23]

Between 1965 and 1973 some 2.6 million Americans in the military served in Vietnam. Keeping this number in mind, this statement puts the number of Vietnam war crimes in perspective, "It is difficult to imagine a comparably populated city in America—or anywhere else—that would not herald the fact that only 278 of its inhabitants had been convicted of 'serious crimes' against its citizenry over an eight-year period."[24]

Oliver Stone's inaccuracy in depicting U.S. soldiers in his movie *Platoon* as sloppy and demoralized impeaches the credibility of any work he has done on the Vietnam War. The movie *Platoon* was based on a platoon that operated near the Cambodian border in 1967. "Oliver Stone also fakes his social history. In 1967, the U.S. forces were not smoking dope and behaving with general indiscipline."[25] Veterans who were in Vietnam during this time period can attest to the fact that morale and lack of discipline were not of the variety that Stone depicts in 1967 and even later in the war. Stone knows this very well, as he served in Vietnam at the time that *Platoon* was depicted. It can only be assumed that Stone used his creative license to make the movie more exciting and marketable.

Another media effort went a long way in depicting the U.S. soldier in Vietnam in a negative light. This was the PBS airing of the series *Vietnam, a Television History.*

In a rebuttal to the PBS series, a videotape called *Television's Vietnam,* Dan Cragg of *Army Magazine* and *National Veterans Review* critiqued the PBS series depiction of the soldier in Vietnam: "I think the great unjustness of this film is that it portrays the American soldier in Vietnam as a drug addict, racial bigot, and a man who murdered his officers and NCOs almost at will. The hundreds of thousands of Americans who went to Vietnam and served honorably and bravely have got to be incensed at this terrible misrepresentation of their bravery and sacrifice on the battlefield."[26]

Platoon and *Full Metal Jacket* also were two of the many movies seen by the U.S. public that had a tendency to depict the American soldier as somewhat incompetent in the face of an "invincible" and elusive enemy. The PBS series seemed to reinforce this perception.

Casualty figures from the war refute this misrepresentation. Far from being invincible, millions of Vietcong and North Vietnamese soldiers were killed or wounded during the war. The kill ratio in the war was massively in favor of the U.S. side.

Kenneth Moorefield of the Vietnam Veterans Leadership Program rebutted the PBS portrayal of the American soldier.

> The distinct impression I had from the series was that the American fighting man and the American army and Armed Services were not the equal of their adversary. The quality of the American fighting man was as high or higher as we've had serving on our behalf in any previous war. . . . I can say that as a former company commander there I . . . I couldn't have received more support from my men. I think they were fantastic . . . they were brave . . . they showed initiative, courage . . . every quality you could possibly hope to have from a soldier in combat.[27]

Charges that U.S. soldiers lost the war due to battlefield incompetence just do not wash. Harry G. Summers Jr. put it this way: "'You know you never beat us on the battlefield,' I told my North Vietnamese (NVA) counterpart, Colonel Tu, during a meeting in Hanoi a week before the fall of Saigon. 'That may be so,' he replied, 'but it is also irrelevant.'"[28] These victories were only irrelevant in the sense they did not lead to overall winning of the war due to a lack of a coherent overall strategy. "But they were not irrelevant in judging the fighting qualities of the American fighting man. Although there are reports that Colonel Tu has recently recanted his too candid comments about American battlefield superiority, other sources corroborate his remark."[29]

Peter Braestrup, who was a combat correspondent for the *New York Times* in Vietnam from 1966 to 1968, wrote his assessment of the U.S. soldier in that war: "American troops, at least until President Nixon began troop withdrawals in 1969, fought as well as (or better than) their elders in World War II or Korea."[30] Braestrup goes on to say: "They were neither victims nor psychopaths (as portrayed in the movie *Platoon*). They were probably better disciplined than their elders; less damage and fewer civilian casualties were inflicted on the South Vietnamese than on the Koreans during the Korean War."[31]

Maj. Gen. George S. Patton (Ret.) wrote his comments concerning the Vietnam soldier in a letter to *Time* magazine. In part he said:

> As a veteran of two wars, Korea and Viet Nam, I can say the Viet Nam soldier far surpassed his Korean War predecessor in overall professionalism and dedication to U.S. objectives. His basic problem was that those objectives were often unclear. This was not the soldier's fault, but he made the best of it. In conclusion, I forward this letter to explain that the characteristics of the leaders portrayed in *Platoon* do not apply to our military forces across the board.[32]

General Patton, as the reader may have surmised, comes from an eminent military background. He spent thirty-three months in Vietnam. He also was regimental commander of the Eleventh Armored Cavalry Regiment in Vietnam.

Military historian Shelby L. Stanton has written of this regiment (nicknamed the Blackhorse Regiment): "The Eleventh Armored Cavalry would become one of the Army's finest units in Vietnam. . . . A series of excellent commanders and aggressive flak-vested cavalrymen would ensure that the 11th ACR gained an enviable combat reputation far out of proportion to their actual numbers."[33] General Patton was one of the finest of the excellent commanders of the Eleventh Armored Cavalry, and his comments about U.S. soldiers in Vietnam have the utmost credibility. He is among the most eminently qualified people to make a judgment of this sort.

Generally speaking, when the media portrayed U.S. soldiers in Vietnam, it was in a negative light. "Seldom is mentioned the good works of soldiers such as Lieutenant Thomas Gray Jr., who were ten thousand times more representative."[34] Gray was the operations officer of a supply and transport battalion. During off-duty time he set up a local orphanage and organized a support network back in Maine to keep the orphanage running. Gray was not satisfied with being responsible for security of his division's base camp, so he maneuvered a way to get himself to a combat unit. Unfortunately, he was killed very soon after he went to the field.[35]

This was just one story, but there were thousands of acts by thousands of U.S. soldiers of kindness, charity, and good works. U.S. veterans who have returned to visit Vietnam in the 1980s and '90s report warmhearted and enthusiastic receptions by the Vietnamese people. These receptions are what is reaped today because of the humanitarian acts and attitudes that were sown by U.S. soldiers during the Vietnam War.

A story told by a group of U.S. veterans who returned to visit Vietnam related that when they first entered certain villages they were treated with suspicion and the villagers were reluctant to associate with them. The villagers at first thought they were Soviets. When they found out they were Americans, the villagers became wildly enthusiastic and friendly. This type of evidence contradicts the image of the American soldier in Vietnam as the barbaric war criminal some would try to perpetuate.

Malignment of Vietnam veterans once they returned to civilian life has existed since the war years and has continued up to the present day. The stereotyped image of the Vietnam veteran as a loser with every conceivable malady had been perpetuated in media works such as *Vietnam, a Television History,* broadcast by PBS, and other media presentations.

William Jayme of the Vietnam Veterans Leadership Program commented on the PBS series' episode number 13, "Legacies": "It seems the image of the veteran is very much the stereotype image of veterans as loser, victim . . . The word they use is haunted. PBS didn't give the other side of the picture which is that veterans are not only well adjusted by and large and productive members of society, but that many vets are now assuming leadership roles in the society."[36]

Others have echoed similar sentiments concerning the truth about the portrayal of Vietnam veterans. " 'The time has come for the public to be made aware that many of us [Vietnam Veterans] are much more successful socially, politically, and economically than the derelict so often stereotyped by the media,' comments William C. Stensland, a former marine who heads a veterans' program in Texas."[37]

Vietnam veteran B.G. Burkett was highly dissatisfied with the stereotypical image of Vietnam veterans. The image included the postwar troubles with depression, alcoholism, domestic problems, and a host of other maladies. Burkett was particularly was successful at exposing fraudulent impostors who were hanging around Vietnam veterans' memorials, fund-raising committees, and even as members of Vietnam veterans' organizations. These individuals could be counted on to be at these places in their jungle fatigues telling tales of woe concerning Vietnam and their experiences. Some of them falsely claimed to be medal winners for their combat experience in Vietnam.

Burkett exposed a man named Jesse Duckworth who was a regular at fund raising activities. Duckworth liked to enthrall reporters with lurid war stories and sign autographs for kids as he stood around in his jungle fatigues outfitted with combat patches. Duckworth liked to claim he was a decorated Green

Beret who had been wounded in Vietnam. "Burkett discovered that Duckworth's official service record showed he had never set foot there. His term of duty, in Germany, had been marred by repeated periods of Absent Without Leave (AWOL)."[38]

Burkett also exposed Joseph Testa Jr., president of the Dallas chapter of the Vietnam Veterans of America (VVA) and also a fixture of the local vet scene. Testa at times wore the Silver Star, which is the army's third-highest award decoration for valor. "But Testa's official record showed he had never won the award. In fact, Testa had never served overseas and nine months of his stateside tour were spent in the stockade."[39]

David Goff, former president of a VVA chapter in Morrisville, N.Y., near Syracuse, is another imposter that Burkett uncovered. Goff, who claimed combat experience in Vietnam, had been treated for PTSD and counseled troubled vets. He had belatedly obtained some of the military's highest awards for valor, including the Distinguished Service Cross, second only to the Medal of Honor. Goff had even persuaded Rep. James Walsh (R., N.Y.) to pin on the medals during an April 1989 ceremony for combat vets. Goff was called a "hero" by the Syracuse *Herald American*.

To Burkett, however, the story of postwar trouble with depression, alcohol, domestic problems and PTSD struck a familiar tone. So did Goff's claim of having been a CIA assassin. Goff's recovery from combat trauma was indeed inspiring, but there was a problem. His service record revealed he had been a clerk in Okinawa and had never set foot in Vietnam.

Yet even when Burkett revealed Goff's deception to the *Herald American,* the newspaper stood by its story, though it, too, had by then obtained Goff's official record.[40]

It is frightening to think that these type of individuals have been the models upon which many Americans have based their image of the Vietnam veteran. It is more frightening that the media has helped to perpetuate this image also, even when presented with evidence of the fraudulence of their subject. It can be speculated that the media desires the image of the Vietnam veteran to be that of the troubled vet in combat fatigues. This image fits the preconceived notion that the media has and probably desires to perpetuate. They seemingly prefer it to be that way, unfortunately.

B.G. Burkett did not limit himself to exposing fraudulent people but also exposed fraudulent ideas and perceptions concerning Vietnam veterans. He used research to reveal some accurate information concerning these veterans.

Concerning the question of a high suicide rate among Vietnam veterans Burkett found: "In 1990, a report in the *American Journal of Psychiatry* refuted claims of a high suicide rate among Vietnam veterans. In fact, government studies reveal they have one of the lowest suicide rates in America—even lower than their non-veteran peers."[41]

Post-Traumatic Stress Disorder (PTSD) is a malady that has been associated with Vietnam veterans. "Burkett learned that PTSD has been blown far out of proportion. More than 2.5 million Americans served in Vietnam, but only 45,000 have received any compensation for exhibiting symptoms, and only 10,000 of those have been severely disabled."[42] This means that fewer than 1 percent have shown any symptoms and fewer than 0.5 percent are disabled due to PTSD.

In terms of unemployment and criminality, "Labor Department research reveals a much higher employment level among Vietnam vets than the national average. Studies also confirm that Vietnam vets have a very low rate of criminality and incarceration."[43] "The evidence is overwhelming that, far from being violent time bombs, Vietnam veterans are among the most well-adjusted groups in America. They are more likely to have higher incomes than those who did not go to Vietnam.

They are also more likely than their peers to own their homes, and they are just as likely to have stable marriages."[44]

The United States needs to realize that Vietnam veterans are all around them. Vietnam veterans exist normally in normal communities. They have normal jobs and normal families, attend normal churches, and send their normal kids to normal schools. Vietnam veterans are farmers, teachers, police officers, fire fighters, doctors, computer analysts, and accountants and in every other occupation. Vietnam veterans are even U.S. senators and representatives. Al Gore, the vice president of the United States, is a Vietnam veteran.

Given all this, as B.G. Burkett has said, "Isn't it time the country recognizes the true face of the Vietnam veteran?"[45]

Unfortunately, there are impediments to recognizing the "true face" of the Vietnam veterans. Foremost of the impediments are the antiwar elements, individuals and institutions such as the media that have a vested interest in distorting what the war was all about.

Draft evaders and other shirkers of duty find it necessary to continuously reiterate the moral superiority of their view of the war as evil to justify their nonparticipation and protest against it. One way to do this is to continue to malign the Vietnam veteran.

Media personalities and the media itself also use malignment of the Vietnam veteran in a fashion similar to the draft-evading individuals and antiwar personalities. The media has very little interest in portraying the Vietnam veteran in a positive light as long as its personnel are dominated by antiwar biases.

I hope a new generation of media personnel will be able to see through the tainted picture of the war and the veteran. That is one of the purposes of this book.

Unfortunately, the following illustration may be indicative of how well a negative image of Vietnam veterans has permeated the collective psyche of America and its media personalities. It deals with a major media personality and a seemingly offhand comment she made concerning Vietnam veterans in 1995. It tends to illustrate the knee-jerk disdain for Vietnam veterans that still permeated broadcast media in 1995.

Katie Couric is co-host of NBC's *Today Show*. On July 27, 1995, the *Today Show* did a segment on the dedication of the new Korean War Veterans Memorial in Washington, D.C. Ms. Couric and NBC used the occasion to get in some jabs at Vietnam veterans one more time.

Readers should keep in mind while reading about this incident the question as to why mention of Vietnam veterans and the Vietnam War was even made on the hallowed occasion of the dedication of a memorial to the killed in action of the Korean War. *Why was it necessary to malign Vietnam veterans in conjunction with this occasion?*

Two Korean War veterans, Col. William Weber and Col. Rosemary McCarthy, were interviewed by Katie Couric on the *Today Show* on July 27, 1995. As part of that interview Ms. Couric stated, "Something like for—more than 54,000 Americans lost their lives. That's nearly as many as lost their lives in—in the Vietnam War, and, of course, this war was over in a much shorter period of time."[46]

Apparently, Ms. Couric was trying to establish some type of comparison with this statement. It could be deduced from this statement that Ms. Couric was attempting to establish that the Korean War was a worse war than the Vietnam War by having more casualties in a much shorter time.

America's combat role in Korea was from 1950 to 1953, a period of three years. America's combat role in Vietnam was from 1965 to 1973, a period of eight years. U.S. battle deaths in Korea were 33,629 and battle deaths in Vietnam were 47,244.[47]

In the three worst years of the Vietnam War, 1967, 1968, and 1969, U.S. combat deaths amounted to 33,384,[48] as compared to Korea's 33,629 in its three years. If an attempt was made to portray the Korean War as significantly worse than the Vietnam War it does not ring true. The two wars were very similar in their severity, as measured by combat casualties.

The next bit of malignment of the Vietnam veteran by Katie Couric and the *Today Show* is a classic example of slur by stealth. Tactics used to jab at Vietnam veterans could only be used by a crafty journalist trying to slant things in a desired direction.

Ms. Couric, during the interview of Korean War veteran Rosemary McCarthy, used a slick ploy to inject her own viewpoint under the guise of asking a question. This tactic has been described as the "I am going to **tell** you a question" method. Ms. Couric said, "Colonel McCarthy, you were an army nurse in the Korean War. I read an interesting column recently that said one of the things that stands out about the—the veterans of the Korean War versus Vietnam veterans, that the Korean veterans were not whiners or complainers. What do you think of that assessment?"[49]

Katie Couric, in a very sly fashion, was able to characterize Vietnam veterans as whiners and complainers on national television. She also was able to get Colonel McCarthy to agree with her. Colonel McCarthy's response to the question of whether this was an accurate assessment was, "Well, I—I don't mind it at all. I think it's true."[50] Whether Colonel McCarthy was agreeing that Korean War veterans were not whiners and complainers or that Vietnam veterans were is not clear, but Ms. Couric and the *Today Show*'s motives are.

The question must be posed again in a different way. *Why did Katie Couric, the* Today Show, *and/or NBC feel compelled to discuss the issue of Vietnam veterans being whiners and complainers on the occasion of the dedication of the Korean War Veterans Memorial?* It can be posited that it was part of the media's continuing penchant, as developed during the Vietnam War, to portray everything possible relating to the war and its veterans in a negative light.

If Katie Couric was not injecting her own views into the matter it would be interesting to have the column that she read and referred to revealed. If it didn't originate with her, it still was written by somebody very recently, which means, as the singing duo Sonny and Cher said, "The beat goes on."

NBC and the *Today Show* were contacted by electronic mail in an attempt to answer questions concerning this matter. Was it scriptwriters, Ms. Couric, or someone else who wanted this interview conducted in this manner? What was the purpose? NBC was informed that, answer or no answer, the matter would be discussed in a book. NBC declined to reply to the questions.

One explanation of the cause of the historic and continuing disparagement of the Vietnam veteran has been offered by Harry G. Summers Jr.:

> While the overwhelming majority of Vietnam veterans have long since returned to civilian life and got on with their lives and careers, many of the draft dodgers and war evaders still struggle with their consciences. Torn by guilt, they continue to try to explain away their evasion by deliberately distorting what the war was all about.
>
> Most veterans could care less about their posturings, but there is one fact that cannot be ignored. In trying to make themselves look good, these shirkers must of necessity make those who did serve look bad.[51]

Many of the shirkers referred to in the preceding are in positions of power and influence today (1996). They have great influence in what the media produces in the form of documentaries and entertainment. Shirkers are in positions of writing and teaching history also. It can be expected that they will continue to write and teach what will be a reaffirmation of their antiwar positions concerning the Vietnam War. The war must be portrayed as incorrect and evil. Whether or not that is true has not been the thrust of this chapter. This chapter has asserted that in order to continue to portray the war as evil, the picture of the warrior has been distorted into a negative portrait. This chapter I hope has given the reader some alternative thoughts to consider concerning this matter.

Notes

1. Jeffrey Hart, "Viet Films Play Games with History," *Herald-Palladium*, Benton Harbor–St. Joseph, Michigan, February 29, 1988, p. 14.
2. Harry G. Summers Jr., "Kindness and Good Works, Not Barbarism and Atrocities Were the Real Hallmarks of the American Military," *Vietnam Magazine*, December 1994, p. 6.
3. Richard L. Wormser, *Three Faces of Vietnam* (New York: Franklin Watts Library, 1993), p. 135.
4. Irwin Unger, *These United States, the Questions of Our Past* (Englewood Cliffs, NJ: Prentice Hall, 1995), p. 856.
5. Paul Boyer, *Todd & Curti's The American Nation* (Austin, TX: Holt, Rhinehart, and Winston, 1995), p. 887.
6. John M. Blum, ed., *The National Experience, a History of the United States* (Fort Worth, TX: Harcourt, Brace, and Jovanovich, 1993), pp. 869–70.
7. Ibid., p. 869.
8. Robert J. Lifton, in Erwi Judith Nies McFadden, ed., *War Crimes and the American Conscience* (New York: Holt, Rhinehart, and Winston, 1970), p. 104, cited in Norman Podhoretz, *Why We Were in Vietnam* (New York: Simon and Schuster, 1982), p. 188.
9. Edward. M. Opton, Jr., Nevitt Sanford, and Robert Cuckles, in *War Crimes and the American Conscience* pp. 113–14, cited in Podhoretz, *Why We Were in Vietnam*, p. 188.
10. Hans J. Morgenthau, in *War Crimes and the American Conscience*, p. 110, cited in Podhoretz, *Why We Were in Vietnam*, p. 188.
11. Podhoretz, *Why We Were in Vietnam*, p. 188.
12. Telford Taylor, *Nuremberg and Vietnam* (New York: Bantam, 1971), p. 139, cited in ibid., p. 188.

13. Daniel Ellsberg, in *War Crimes and the American Conscience,* p. 130, cited in Podhoretz, *Why We Were in Vietnam,* p. 188.
14. A. Francis Hatch, "One Despicable Legacy of the Vietnam War Is the False Portrayals of American Soldiers as Bloodthirsty Barbarians," *Vietnam Magazine,* August 1995, p. 60.
15. Guenter Lewy, *America in Vietnam* (New York: Oxford University Press, 1978), p. 224.
16. Podhoretz, *Why We Were in Vietnam,* p. 181.
17. Lewy, *America in Vietnam,* p. 224.
18. Podhoretz, *Why We Were in Vietnam,* p. 181.
19. Ibid., p. 182.
20. Lewy, *America in Vietnam,* p. 317, cited in Podhoretz, *Why We Were in Vietnam,* p. 182.
21. Podhoretz, *Why We Were in Vietnam,* p. 182.
22. Malcolm McConnell, "The True Face of the Vietnam Vet," *Readers Digest,* May 1994, p. 129.
23. Harry G. Summers Jr., *Vietnam War Almanac* (New York: Facts on File, 1985), p. 91.
24. Hatch, "One Despicable Legacy," p. 60.
25. Hart, "Viet Films Play Games with History," p. 14.
26. Dan Cragg, videotape, *Television's Vietnam* (Washington, DC: Accuracy in Media, 1985).
27. Kenneth Moorefield, *Television's Vietnam,* 1985.
28. Harry G. Summers Jr., "Deliberate Distortions Still Obscure Understanding of the Vietnam War. It's Time They Were Laid to Rest," *Vietnam Magazine,* August 1989, p. 59.
29. Ibid.
30. Peter Braestrup, in Bill McCloud, *What Should We Tell Our Children about Vietnam?* (Norman: University of Oklahoma Press, 1989), p. 17.
31. Ibid.
32. George S. Patton III, "Letters to the Editor," *Time Magazine,* March 23, 1987, pp. 7–8.
33. Shelby L. Stanton, *The Rise and Fall of an American Army, U.S. Ground Forces in Vietnam, 1965-1973* (Novato, CA: Presidio, 1985), p. 78.
34. Summers, "Kindness and Good Works, Not Barbarism," p. 6.
35. Ibid.
36. William Jayme, *Television's Vietnam* (Washington, DC: Accuracy in Media, 1985).
37. Wendell S. Merrick, *U.S. News and World Report,* March 29, 1982, in David L. Bender, *The Vietnam War, Opposing Viewpoints* (St. Paul, MN: Greenhaven, 1984), p. 115.
38. McConnell, "The True Face of the Vietnam Vet," pp. 127–28.
39. Ibid.

40. Ibid., p. 129.
41. Ibid.
42. Ibid.
43. Ibid., p. 130.
44. Ibid.
45. Ibid.
46. Katie Couric, NBC, *Today Show,* July, 27, 1995.
47. Summers, *Vietnam War Almanac,* p. 112.
48. Shelby L. Stanton, *Vietnam Order of Battle* (Millwood, NY: Kraus, 1986), p. 349.
49. Couric.
50. Ibid.
51. Harry G. Summers Jr., "Deliberate Distortions Still Obscure Understanding of the Vietnam War. It's Time They Were Laid to Rest," *Vietnam Magazine,* August 1989, p. 58.

12

Antiwar

To have a thorough understanding of the many facets of the Vietnam War it is necessary to have an understanding of the antiwar movement also. This movement attracted a broad range of people with a variety of ideas and types of reasoning. The movement challenged the U.S. government's right to pursue the Vietnam War with a tenacity that was unprecedented in scale and duration in the annals of U.S. history.

This chapter will present analysis of the antiwar movement. What the movement stood for will be presented and analyzed as well as the movement's perceptions of the war and U.S. participation in it. Some of the misperceptions of the antiwar movement will be explored as well, and part of this analysis will be done by former antiwar people who have changed their views as time has passed.

The movement's perceived impact on the war as well as counterarguments from other sources giving a differing perception of the movement's impact on the war will also be explored. Central to this will be the argument as to whether the antiwar movement shortened American participation in the war or actually strengthened the enemy's resolve and lengthened the war instead.

The sincerity of the movement's commitment to real peace will be discussed as well as an analysis of the "dangers" that antiwar youths faced. How much were they putting on the line to protest the war?

While not all-encompassing of the subjects to be covered in this chapter, this introduction will serve as a springboard to an analysis of the antiwar movement during the Vietnam War. I hope it will contribute to a greater understanding of the war itself and the social milieu of its era.

While not going into a history of it origins and its political platform prior to the Vietnam War, the group most closely associated with the antiwar movement was the Students for a Democratic Society (SDS). The views of the SDS on the Vietnam War will be discussed to show one of the viewpoints the antiwar movement took on the issue of the war in Vietnam. A high school textbook, *Todd & Curti's The American Nation,* describes the SDS this way:

> Though it was only one of many groups opposing the war, in the minds of many Americans, the SDS *was* the antiwar movement. At colleges across the United States, the SDS and other student groups and faculty members held antiwar rallies and debates. These groups particularly criticized the involvement of universities in research and development for the military. They also protested the draft, the presence of the Reserve Officers Training Corps (ROTC) on campus, and the recruitment efforts by the armed services, the CIA, and such defense contractors as Dow Chemical, the manufacturer of napalm.[1]

This was the only reference to the SDS made in this high school textbook. A student reading the material in *Todd & Curti's The American Nation* receives a very sanitized version of the SDS. Later during the war, this group turned to violent, confrontational methods as a method of protest concerning the war.

As mentioned, the SDS was the dominant representative of the antiwar movement and some of its expressed views will follow. In 1965 the SDS stated that "the war is fundamentally a civil war, waged by South Vietnamese against their govern-

213

ment; it is not a 'war of aggression.' Military assistance from North Vietnam and China has been minimal."[2] The question of whether the war was a civil war or an invasion from the North has been previously examined in chapter 6. Dominant opinion in the antiwar movement was obviously on the side of the civil war thesis.

The SDS also stated in 1965 that "it is a hideously immoral war. America is committing pointless murder."[3] They also stated at that time: "We urge the participation of all students who agree with us that the war in Vietnam injures both Vietnamese and Americans, and should be stopped."[4]

As time passed and the war continued, the rhetoric of the SDS became more strident and militant. In a policy statement issued in 1969, the SDS showed its more radical side: "What's new is that today not quite so many people are confused, and a lot more people are angry; angry about the fact that the promises we have heard since first grade are all jive; angry that, when you get down to it, this system is nothing but the total economic and military put-down of the oppressed peoples of the world."[5]

Making common bond with the enemy in Vietnam, the SDS also said in the policy statement: "Our actions showed the Vietnamese that there were masses of young people in this country facing the same enemy that they faced."[6] Their stance was that the U.S. government was the common enemy of the Vietnamese communists and the SDS. The actions the SDS referred to were the riots and confrontation that had occurred at the Democratic National Convention in Chicago during the summer of 1968.

The SDS called for a return to Chicago in 1969 for an anniversary demonstration of sorts. They described it this way:

> But it will be a different action. An action not only against a single war or a "foreign policy," but against the whole imperialist

system that made the war a necessity. An action not only for immediate withdrawal of all U.S. occupation troops, but in support of the heroic fight of the Vietnamese people and the National Liberation Front for freedom and independence. An action not only to bring "peace to Vietnam," but beginning to establish another front against imperialism right here in America—to "bring the war home."[7]

No longer was this segment of the antiwar movement content to demand U.S. withdrawal from the Vietnam War. It crossed the line of objecting to U.S. policy to siding with the enemy. For those not well versed in these matters SDS rhetoric also was attacking the capitalist system of U.S. society. They were vowing to wage war against the American system while declaring support for its foes: "We are expressing total support for the National Liberation Front and the newly formed *Provisional Revolutionary Government of South Vietnam.*"[8] Both the NLF and the PRG were the communists of South Vietnam.

Another U.S. high school textbook, *American Voices, a History of the United States, 1865 to the Present,* informs its young readers: "SDS was not, as some charged, a communist organization. Most of its members deplored the oppressive nature of communist regimes throughout the world. It was sympathetic to many Marxist ideas, however, including the idea that working classes were the key to creating social change."[9]

Rhetoric of the SDS sounded suspiciously similar to communist rhetoric. They sided with the communists in Vietnam. Since they deplored the "oppressive nature" of communist regimes throughout the world, the question must be posed as to how they felt about the oppressive communist regime installed by the Vietnamese from the North after the war ended. Do former members of the SDS still believe that the war was a simple civil war and later a war against U.S. imperialists?

Jane Fonda was a well-known activist during the Vietnam

War. She was married and then later divorced from SDS founder Tom Hayden. Ms. Fonda engaged in many antiwar activities, including traveling to the enemy capital of Hanoi and making anti-American propaganda broadcasts and films. During the war it was her stance that efforts by her and the antiwar movement would shorten the war. She still maintained that stance and perspective many years later, as evidenced in an interview with Barbara Walters on ABC's *20/20* in 1988. Ms. Fonda said in that interview, "I feel that . . . those of us who . . . who opposed the war, including those who went to Hanoi and . . . and brought back documented information about what was going on . . . that wasn't getting out . . . that we helped end the war . . . that . . . and what that meant was that the POWs came home sooner . . . that the killing stopped sooner."[10]

Ms. Fonda's stance and that of many in the antiwar movement will later be challenged. Others will contend that the antiwar movement and its actions actually lengthened the war.

"The vast majority of antiwar activists were liberals, leftists, and pacifists who argued for the earliest possible cessation of fighting and a negotiated settlement on the assumption that peace was the preferred way of resolving the political problems of Indochina."[11] These people worked for the goal of what they saw as peace and a U.S. withdrawal.

There was, however, a more sinister element to the antiwar movement: "But a small minority of social radicals and war resisters believed that liberation was at least as important as peace, and that the two values could not be vindicated in Indochina until the U.S. withdrew and the revolutionaries triumphed."[12] This element of the antiwar movement was dedicated to U.S. withdrawal *and* a communist victory in Vietnam. As shown earlier, groups like the SDS fell into the latter category. These groups made common cause with the enemy that the United States was fighting and was willing to use violence against the U.S. power structure to achieve their end.

Nonstudent, nonyouth efforts in the antiwar movement were expressed also. A group of 158 professors, clergy, authors, and members of various other segments of the antiwar movement signed and published *"A Call to Resist Illegitimate Authority."* This statement contained within in it the following: "Many of us believe that open resistance to the war and the draft is the course of action most likely to strengthen the moral resolve with which all of us can oppose the war and most likely bring an end to the war."[13]

David Stockman, who later was the U.S. representative to Congress from the Fourth District of Michigan and Pres. Ronald Reagan's director of the Office of Management and Budget, was a leader in the University Christian Movement's (UCM's) antiwar activities at Michigan State University during the Vietnam War.

The UCM and Stockman at times found themselves allied with the more radical SDS. At one point Stockman defended the SDS as true U.S. patriots in a speech rebutting the SDS as un-American.[14] Stockman said:

A nation is not defined by the particular policy, of a particular administration, in power at a particular point in time. Rather, the genius of a nation is expressed in those lofty ideals and broad spiritual currents which have threaded their way through the fabric of its history. In our country these ideals are embodied in concepts like: distributive justice, limited government; individual freedom of speech, assembly and worship; and the rights to life, liberty and the pursuit of happiness . . . Many of us feel that American intervention in Vietnam runs contrary to the spirit of this historical tradition. Therefore, our commitment to the real core values and ideals that have made this nation great demands we oppose the war.

There have been many expressions of this opposition. One of them being the SDS anti-draft union . . . I think the action of many of those . . . is motivated by a broader courage than simple, blind obedience, and by a sense of responsibility to values higher than the shallow rhetoric of the present administration.[15]

Not only did Mr. Stockman make common cause with the SDS, but also he basically argued that those who resisted the draft, such as the SDS antidraft union, did so out of higher moral courage than those who did not. The implication is that those who allowed themselves to be drafted did so out of "blind obedience." Mr. Stockman obviously viewed the war as contrary to America's best interests and historical values. Resistance to the Vietnam War and the draft apparently then would be the way to end U.S. participation in this war.

Thomas Greer represents another slant on the antiwar movement. Greer and other clergy convened what was called the Interfaith Convocation on War and Peace in East Lansing in January and February of 1967. Greer's view of the war in Vietnam was that it undermined America's image in the world as peace-loving and made it more likely that the United States would have a nuclear confrontation with China and Russia.[16]

It was not too long after the Convocation that the University Christian Movement's regional headquarters endorsed national wars of liberation. They, too, crossed the line and made common cause with America's enemy in Vietnam. Apparently David Stockman agreed:

Since the regional UCM had developed an interpretation of the Vietnam War somewhat similar to that of the national SDS, though the former was more concerned with the threat of Marxist dictatorships than the latter, MSU, SDS, and UCM began to coordinate their antiwar activities. Kindman, Price, Stockman, and thirty-nine other activists placed an advertisement in *The Paper* stating their intention to refuse to fight in Vietnam and to encourage others to do likewise.[17]

218

"Michigan State SDSers in 1966 established the first campus-based underground newspaper in American History, *The Paper*."[18] MSU UCM activist David Stockman attended SDS meetings and wrote for the *Paper*.[19]

The antiwar story is well-known since its actions have been well publicized and its story has been adequately told. Using the positions of Hayden, Stockman, and Fonda was an attempt to refresh memories of where the movement stood. They are also good subjects as they became well-known persons in mainstream society, Jane Fonda of course through her business efforts such as exercise videos and movies and Stockman through achieving brief national prominence in politics. Hayden is a politician in California state politics, having had his national political aspirations thwarted somewhat. All three are active in the mainstream America that they deplored to different degrees at an earlier stage of their lives.

A story not as well told is that of second thoughts concerning the antiwar movement and its impact on the war. Some of the protestors themselves now see things differently, and that is a story that also needs to be told. Added to this, there are other viewpoints concerning the antiwar movement that need to be examined from a variety of sources knowledgeable of the Vietnam War.

There are certain myths concerning the antiwar movement that developed during the war and have been perpetuated in history. "One myth, promoted by activists and liberal scholars, is that antiwar protest, its base on the nation's campuses, compelled U.S. foreign policy makers to end our military participation in the Vietnam conflict."[20] "The antiwar opposition constrained Washington's waging of the war. But it could neither stop the violence in Vietnam, nor overcome the mystique that Vietnam was vital to American security and basic to Nixon's promised 'generation of peace.'"[21]

John E. Mueller, professor of political science at the University of Rochester, remarked about the antiwar movement: "Washington was certainly aware of the protests. But the Johnson administration's about-faces in 1968—stopping the bombing of North Vietnam and ending our troop escalation—had more to do with disaffection within the Government itself over how badly the war was going and its high costs."[22]

Prof. Mueller also says that there was a change in attitude in the government in 1968. China's engulfment in its own cultural revolution and Indonesia's destruction of its Communist Party caused this assessment: "The value of saving Vietnam from Communism had gone down since we got committed in 1965."[23]

The antiwar movement had always considered President Johnson's near defeat by antiwar senator Eugene McCarthy a great victory for the peace movement. "Mr. Mueller also points out that President Johnson's near defeat by Senator Eugene McCarthy in the New Hampshire primary, which influenced President Johnson's decision not to run again, was caused more by angry hawks than by doves. At the ballot box, anti-Johnson hawks outnumbered anti-Johnson doves by 3 to 2."[24] It could be concluded that the New Hampshire primary was a message to the government that it wanted the war militarily won, not the negotiated peace and withdrawal that the antiwar movement wanted.

Mueller also argues that the protestors' actions assured Richard Nixon victory in two presidential elections. Attacks by the protestors on Hubert Humphrey, Democratic candidate for president in 1968, probably gave Nixon his slim margin in that election. Having the Democratic convention in 1972 controlled by opponents of the war resulted in George McGovern garnering that party's nomination. McGovern's nomination, a terrible choice by the Democrats in 1972, led to a landslide victory for Nixon.[25] Helping the relatively hawkish Richard Nixon get elected did not hasten the end of U.S. military involvement in Vietnam.

There are many others who feel that the antiwar movement helped lengthen the war, as opposed to making it end sooner. Vietnam veteran and author James A. Webb falls into this category: "I think they *extended* it."[26] Webb continues:

> You create the wrong kind of strain, confront the people who are in authority, encourage the North Vietnamese, and the war drags on. *They* had no need to negotiate. The negotiating was being done for them on the streets of Washington. When the Indochina Peace Campaign began in 1973, Jane Fonda was in *Hanoi*. That's why, in my opinion, the war went on. Lord knows how many . . . I don't want to put a number on it.[27]

"How many" referred to the amount of Americans killed because of the antiwar movement. "At one seminar, Webb stated flatly that the peace movement resulted in the death of several thousand more Americans."[28]

Henry Kissinger, adviser to the President, felt the antiwar movement affected America's position during negotiations in Paris to end the war: "No meeting with the North Vietnamese was complete without a recitation of the statements of our domestic opposition."[29] He also said of the war protestors: "They were, in my view, as wrong as they were passionate. Their pressures delayed the end of the war, not accelerated it; their simplifications did not bring closer the peace, of the yearning for which they had no monopoly."[30]

Dean Rusk, former secretary of state during the Johnson administration, commented on the antiwar movement, "So I think that those dissenters in this country . . . whatever their motivations . . . in effect said to Hanoi . . . just hang in there, gentlemen, and you will win politically what you could not win militarily."[31]

221

Arkady Shevchenko, a former Soviet diplomat, recalled something that had been said by former Soviet premier Yuri Andropov, "As Andropov once mentioned at a politburo meeting at which I was present . . . 'the war would be won not in Vietnam but . . . in the streets of American cities.'"[32]

Gen. H. Norman Schwarzkopf of Desert Storm fame had also been involved in the Vietnam War. During his first tour in Vietnam he was attached to a South Vietnamese Airborne unit and that unit had overrun a Vietcong headquarters. Among the documents they captured had been a directive from Ho Chi Minh that said in effect: "I know you are facing more and more Americans right now, but don't worry. We're going to win the war against America the same way we won the war against the French: not on the battlefield, but in the enemy's homeland."[33] This bit of confidence was expressed by Ho Chi Minh in 1965, the beginning of the U.S. buildup.

Confidence in the antiwar movement's impact by the enemy continued to build as the movement reached its peak in the United States: "As a result, the Vietnamese Communists had become convinced that it was their agents in the United States who had been successful in leading the movement and in forcing the U.S. government to enter into negotiations to end the war. VCP officials used to declare that they would defeat the Americans in Washington D.C., just as they had the French in Paris in 1954."[34]

The foregoing definitely shows a differing perspective of the antiwar movement's impact on the Vietnam War. Readers should be able to make a more balanced judgment as to whether the movement shortened or lengthened the Vietnam War.

It has already been demonstrated that some of the segments of the antiwar movement were not content with the withdrawal of U.S. forces. Certain segments of the movement desired to see a victory by the other side. These elements of the movement believed that a victory by the NLF would result in a better situation in Vietnam than the type of scenario favored by the U.S. government. The SDS had taken this position. This point of view was articulated by antiwar activist Ronald Radosh:

> We regarded the Vietnamese war as a simple liberation struggle against the American aggressor. Therefore we responded with hostility to the suggestion that the Communists might be enemies of freedom, or that a Communist victory in Vietnam might be worse for the Vietnamese themselves. To us, the Vietcong were progressive allies, and all anti-Communists our reactionary enemies. We held that anti-Communism was simply a mask for counter-revolution, and we sided with the anti-imperialist revolutionaries of the Third World.[35]

As time passed, many of the antiwar radicals changed their views concerning the Vietnam War. Views espoused during the war have been transformed into a different perspective about the situation in Vietnam.

During the war Peter Collier had this perspective: "We saw the Victcong as more than a guerrilla force. They were also an all-purpose metaphor for the power of the individual against the bullet headed technocrats like Defense Secretary Robert MacNamara, who ran The Machine."[36] Once the Vietnam War was over, Collier related, "It didn't take long for the utopia we of the Left had predicted for Southeast Asia—once the United States was defeated—to reveal itself as a nightmare of tiger cages, boat people, and political re-education camps."[37]

Peter L. Berger was part of a group called Clergy and Laymen Concerned about Vietnam (CALCAV). His view in 1967 was: "All sorts of dire results might well follow a reduction or a withdrawal of the American engagement in Vietnam. Morally speaking, however, it is safe to assume that none of these could be worse than what is taking place right now."[38] By 1980,

Berger said, "well, it was *not* safe to assume . . . I was wrong and so were all those who thought as I did . . . contrary to what most members (including myself) of the antiwar expected, the peoples of Indochina have, since 1975, been subjected to suffering far worse than anything that was inflicted on them by the United States and its allies."[39]

Michael Medved said as an antiwar crusader, "Our enemies in Vietnam were motivated by nationalism, not Communism; warnings of a 'bloodbath' following an American withdrawal from Southeast Asia were groundless McCarthyite scare tactics."[40] After the war Medved changed his assessment: "As events unfolded, and reports of widespread suffering and bloodshed became harder and harder to deny, I felt that those of us that had participated in the antiwar movement had a moral obligation to admit that we had been profoundly wrong concerning the postwar future of Southeast Asia and the nature of the Vietnamese and Cambodian Communists."[41]

Another member of the antiwar movement, Jeffrey Herf, said during the war, "I shared in the radical conviction that a Vietnamese communist victory would be preferable to continuation of the war."[42] Once the war was over, Mr. Herf saw things differently. He said: "The Communists were every bit as bad as American supporters of the war said they would be. . . . Our greatest political misjudgment concerning the war was to believe that Vietnamese Communism would bring a better society to South Vietnam."[43]

David Stockman, former congressman, U.S. budget director, and antiwar activist on the MSU campus discussed earlier in this book, has also modified his views on the war: "Then I thought there was no U.S. interest involved. Now I think there was in the abstract. Then I thought it was an entirely indigenous nationalist uprising. Now I think it was exploited from Hanoi. The way we conducted it and managed it was a mistake—but not because it was wrong to be there."[44]

Citing these examples of antiwar protestors changing their minds is not intended to imply that they are representative of the whole antiwar movement or even a majority of it. It would be difficult to obtain a representative sample of these people and ascertain how they feel about the movement at this later date. What the listing of these examples is intended to do is give a different perspective of the antiwar movement from some people who are in a unique position to comment on it.

In 1994, a Marxist historian, Eugene Genovese, criticized the antiwar movement during the Vietnam War: "In a trenchant polemic that appears in the summer issue of the leftist quarterly *Dissent* (est. circ. 10,000), Genovese argues that many American radicals were, in effect, accomplices to mass murder. Many U.S. advocates of a Viet Cong victory in Vietnam, for example, have never accepted that what they considered a radical egalitarian democracy was in fact a cruel totalitarian dictatorship."[45]

Criticism from Genovese was somewhat unique. The words that were used might have just as well been uttered by right-wing militarists. Instead these criticism were leveled by an avowed Marxist, from the left side of the political spectrum. It was this left side that was most critical of U.S. involvement in the Vietnam War.

Tom Hayden, founder of the SDS and antiwar movement leader, suggested at one time that there be a memorial recognizing the courage and sacrifices as well as the altruism of members of the antiwar movement. Seemingly, Mr. Hayden would like to equate the war protestors' sacrifice with that of those who served in the Vietnam War.

"During the Vietnam War, over half a million men committed draft violations that could have sent them to prison for five years."[46] Statistics belie the notion that these draft violators really faced much danger, as only a fraction of them ever faced prison for their actions. "Fewer than half of the 570,000 who

225

committed draft violations were reported to federal prosecutors—and only 25,000 of them were indicted. Fewer than 9,000 were convicted and just 3,250 went to prison, most of whom were paroled within a year."[47]

Former protestor Michael Medved put it this way:

> To be sure, a tiny minority of movement activists paid a practical price for their beliefs, going to jail rather than registering for the draft or finding new homes in Canada or Sweden. But for the overwhelming majority of anti-Vietnam protesters—including nearly all of us involved in leadership positions in the movement—our work against the war required little risk. It was, in fact, glamorous, satisfying, and fun. Anyone who participated in a major demonstration will fondly recall the electric atmosphere, the intoxicating sense of shared purpose and comradeship. . . .
>
> Our sacrifices, Mr. Hayden? Should we console ourselves over the football games and parties we missed? The Bob Dylan albums we might have bought—but didn't because we invested in bus fare to Washington or Chicago? Could anyone seriously suggest that our suffering be compared with that of the men who gave their lives and their health in the jungles of Southeast Asia?[48]

Author James Webb referred to Allenwood Prison and downplayed even the sacrifice of those who went to jail. He said: "There weren't any VC at Allenwood."[49]

Discussing the courage of the members of the antiwar movement in 1975, author and antiwar activist James Fallows said, "It is clear that if the men of Harvard had wanted to do the very most they could to shorten the war, they should have been drafted or imprisoned en masse."[50] His argument was that as long as the death notices from Vietnam were going to poor neighborhoods in urban and rural areas the mothers from the rich neighborhoods were not on their telephones screaming at their congressmen and writing letters to the president about an evil war that killed their sons or ruined their careers by sending them to prison for resisting the draft.[51]

> One of Fallows' most penetrating self-criticisms was that while those in the antiwar movement (of which he was a part) convinced themselves they were the "sand in the gears of the great war machine" by burning their draft cards and marching, the real war—the courageous way—to have ended the war would have been to *go* to war.[52]

> Draft resistance . . . Leaders set 100,000 acts of resistance as their goal after *New York Times* columnist Tom Wicker wrote: "If the Johnson administration had to prosecute 100,000 Americans in order to maintain authority, its real power to pursue the Vietnamese war would be crippled if not destroyed." Such large-scale revolt never materialized. Few students heeded the call to drop their deferments, and inductees continued to flee to Canada rather than face jail.[53]

As for the militant SDS, "at a national SDS conference only one-fifth of the mostly college-age delegates supported a plan to renounce their deferments. Antiwar leaders were 'frankly appalled' at the fear of alienating students by raising the college deferment issue."[54] Apparently it was most convenient to be against the war in a relatively safe, noncommittal fashion.

Some have questioned the sincerity of the antiwar movement. Was it really against the Vietnam War, or was it spearheaded mainly by those who were trying to prevent their individual participation in the war?

Prior to 1967 the white middle-class had not been massively threatened with massive participation in the war via the draft. These people had been able to procure the safety of college deferments. The war was a remote occurrence for them.

By 1967 many of these students were ready to graduate. Simultaneously, the war was widening and these graduates were beginning to be called on to serve in much larger numbers. "The threat of being conscripted for a war that was the object of widespread moral revulsion made marchers and shouters out of young men who might have been less concerned over victimization of an Asian people and the turning into cannon fodder of farm boys and the sons of the working class and the minorities."[55]

As the war widened for the United States and the draft became a bigger threat, the protests widened. The converse also became true as Pres. Richard Nixon Vietnamized the brutality of the war. Lower draft calls reduced the intensity of protest as the threat of going to war was reduced and the draft lottery allowed men to know that they would not have to serve. Finally draft calls stopped in 1972 and the United States reverted to an all-volunteer military. All of this diffused the antiwar movement.

It did not diffuse the brutality of the Vietnam War, however. "It may seem strange at first glance that the most brutal attack of the entire war—the notorious Christmas bombing of 1972—generated hardly a ripple of protest from America's universities."[56] When it is placed in proper context it becomes easier to understand: "Our silence is easily understood, however, when one takes note of the fact that draft calls came to an end at precisely that same moment in history—December 1972. By removing our own tender bodies from the line of fire, in other words, President Nixon significantly dimmed our heroic concern for the suffering masses of Southeast Asia."[57]

The antiwar movement was never a majority. Students playing an active political role in it were a minority. In 1972, eighteen-year-olds were given the right to vote for the first time. Coupled with this, there was a candidate, George McGovern, who said he would remove all U.S. troops from Vietnam on the first day he took office if elected. The antiwar movement had a golden opportunity to display its overwhelming antipathy for the Vietnam War and flex its muscle politically. This did not occur. Only a very small percentage of college students bothered to vote in the 1972 presidential election, at a time when the Vietnam War was supposed to be a dominant issue on U.S. college campuses.

The U.S. voting public must not have seen immediate withdrawal from Vietnam as a priority either. They elected Richard Nixon in a landslide. George McGovern's stance on Vietnam was seemingly repudiated, and Richard Nixon's Vietnamization policy was seemingly given a vote of confidence by the U.S. electorate.

All of this points to the conclusion that it is possible that the antiwar movement was but a vociferous minority and did not necessarily reflect mainstream U.S. public opinion. The emphasis it was given in the media then and the nostalgic but pseudo-historical presentation in a variety of media forms it has been given in succeeding years very likely may be overblown. It is hoped that the examination that has been undertaken here will provide a degree of balance and understanding of the antiwar movement during the Vietnam War.

Notes

1. Paul Boyer, *Todd & Curti's The American Nation* (Austin, TX: Holt, Rhinehart, and Winston, 1995), p. 876.
2. Students for a Democratic Society, "A Call to All Students to March on Washington to End the War in Vietnam, April 17, 1965," collection of George Katsiaficas, in *Vietnam: A Visual Investigation* (CD-ROM) (Redmond, WA: Medio Multimedia, 1994).
3. Ibid.
4. Ibid.
5. Students for a Democratic Society, "Bring the War Home!," collection of George Katsiaficas, in *Vietnam: A Visual Investigation.*
6. Ibid.

7. Ibid.
8. Ibid.
9. Carol Berkin et al., *American Voices, a History of the United States, 1865 to the Present* (Glenview, IL: Scott Foresman, 1995), p. 787.
10. Jane Fonda, interview with Barbara Walters on ABC's *20/20,* June 3, 1988.
11. Charles DeBenedetti, *Peace Heroes in Twentieth Century America* (Bloomington: Indiana University Press, 1986), p. 15.
12. Ibid.
13. N. L. Zaroulis, *Who Spoke Up? American Protest against the War in Vietnam* (New York: Holt, Rhinehart, and Winston, 1985), p. 130.
14. Kenneth J. Heineman, *The Peace Movement at American State Universities in the Vietnam Era* (New York: New York University Press, 1993), p. 89.
15. Ibid.
16. Ibid., p. 141.
17. Ibid., pp. 141–42.
18. Ibid., p. 6.
19. Ibid., p. 139.
20. Ibid., p. 2.
21. DeBenedetti, *Peace Heroes,* p. 16.
22. John E. Mueller, *War, Presidents and Public Opinion* (1973), in Fox Butterfield, "The New Vietnam Scholarship," *New York Times Magazine,* February 13, 1983, p. 60.
23. Ibid.
24. Ibid.
25. Ibid.
26. Myra MacPherson, *Long Time Passing, Vietnam and the Haunted Generation* (New York: Doubleday, 1984), p. 546.
27. Ibid.
28. Ibid.
29. Henry Kissinger, *White House Years* (Boston, MA: Little, Brown, 1979), p. 1041.
30. Ibid., p. 510.
31. Dean Rusk, ABC News Special *45-85,* May 7, 1985.
32. Arkady Shevchenko, ABC News Special, *45-85.*
33. H. Norman Schwarzkopf, *It Doesn't Take a Hero* (New York: Bantam, 1992), p. 181.
34. Nguyen Van Canh, *Vietnam under Communism 1975–1982* (Stanford, CA: Hoover Institution Press, 1985), p. 258.
35. Ronald Radosh, "Hanging Up the Old Red Flag," in Peter Collier and David Horowitz, eds., *Second Thoughts, Former Radicals Look Back at the Sixties* (New York: Madison, 1989), p. 14.

36. Peter Collier, "At Home: The Left's Anti-War Follies," *American Legion Magazine*, February 1993.
37. Ibid.
38. Peter L. Berger, "Indochina and the American Conscience," Commentary, February 1980, in Norman Podhoretz, *Why We Were in Vietnam* (New York: Oxford University Press, 1978), p. 197.
39. Ibid., pp. 197–98.
40. Michael Medved, "Ironies of a Political Decade," in Collier and Horowitz, *Second Thoughts*, pp. 19–20.
41. Ibid., p. 22.
42. Jeffrey Herf, "When I Hear the Word 'Movement,'" in Collier and Horowitz, *Second Thoughts*, p. 41.
43. Ibid., p. 42.
44. MacPherson, *Long Time Passing*, p. 163.
45. Eugene Genovese, quoted in John Elson, "In Search of Apologies," *Time*, August 22, 1994, p. 87.
46. MacPherson, *Long Time Passing*, p. 380.
47. M. Lawrence Baskir and William A. Strauss, *Chance and Circumstance: The Draft, the War, and the Vietnam Generation* (New York: Alfred A. Knopf, 1978), cited in ibid.
48. Michael Medved, "60's Generation Shouldn't Be So Smug," *Wall Street Journal*, April 28, 1986, p. 22.
49. MacPherson, *Long Time Passing*, p. 547.
50. James Fallows, "What Did You Do in the Class War, Daddy?" *Washington Monthly*, 1975, cited in Christopher Buckley, "Viet Guilt, Were the Real Prisoners of War the Young Americans Who Never Left Home?" *Esquire*, September 1983, p. 70.
51. Ibid.
52. Ibid.
53. MacPherson, *Long Time Passing*, p. 381.
54. Ibid.
55. Ibid., p. 717.
56. Medved, "60's Generation," p. 22.
57. Ibid.

Index

Acheson, Dean, 18
Adams, Eddie, 166–67
Andropov, Yuri, 222
Ap Bac, Battle of, 37
Army of the Republic of Vietnam
   (ARVN), 141

Bao Dai, 17, 18, 32
Burkett, B.G., 202, 204

C. Turner Joy, 48, 49
Cambodia, 72, 146
Channel One, 175
Christmas bombings, 75, 160–62
Churchill, Winston, 5, 6
Clifford, Clark, 135, 137
Comintern, 91, 94
Containment, 8
Cooper, Anderson, 175
Couric, Katie, 206–08
Cronkite, Walter, 69, 131, 133, 162,
   175

Democratic Republic of Vietnam
   (DRV) 18, 26
Denton, Jeremiah, 166
DESOTO patrols, 46
Dien Bien Phu, 20–21, 24
Domino Theory, 22, 28–29, 40
Dulles, John Foster, 25
Duong Quiynh Hoa (Dr.), 121, 129
Duong Van Minh, 78

Easter Offensive, 74
Eisenhower, Dwight D., 25
Eleventh Armored Cavalry Regiment,
   152, 200
Ellsberg, Daniel, 194

Fonda, Jane, 216, 221

general uprising, 69, 126
Geneva Accords, 24, 61, 62, 104
Genovese, Eugene, 225
Goldwater, Barry, 166
Gulf of Tonkin Resolution, 41, 44,
   50–52, 53
Gulf of Tonkin Incident, 41, 47–49

Hart, Jeffrey, 191
Hayden, Tom, 216, 225
Ho Chi Minh, 14, 15, 16, 17, 18, 27,
   87—, 107, 111
Ho Chi Minh Trail, 66
Huntley, Chet, 132

Ia Drang Valley Battle, 178

Johnson, Lyndon, 31, 37, 55, 71,
   135
Joint Chiefs of Staff (JCS), 136

Kennan, George, 8
Kennedy, John F., 33
Kent State University, 147, 153
Khe Sanh, 127, 133
Khruschev, Nikita, 35, 36
Kim Phuc, Phan, 169–71
Kissinger, Henry, 72, 75, 183
Korean War, 12–14
Kovic, Ron, 191

Le Duan, 99, 119
Le Duc Tho, 75, 119
Lee Kuan Yew, 187
Liddy, G. Gordon, 131